RANDOM⁽¹⁾ THOUGHTS
FOR A RANDOM⁽²⁾ GENERATION

By Dana Kramer

(1)Random: Made, done and chosen at random
(2)Random: Without definite aim or direction

All Scripture quotations unless otherwise indicated, are taken from the New King James Version®. Copyright © 1982 by Thomas Nelson, Inc. Used by permission. All rights reserved.

2016 Dana Kramer, all rights reserved.

Printed in the United State of America

TABLE OF CONTENTS

INTRODUCTION 5
LIVING STONES 8
THE SCOFFING SYNDROME 14
THE IMAGE 20
HE'S LOOKING FOR FRUIT 25
THE MOST MISINTERPRETED SCRIPTURE EVER. .29
THE STUPID ROOM 32
THE HELPER 36
THE LION 42
YOU DO NOT KNOW WHAT YOU ASK 50
REWARDS 56
THE WORLD IS SUFFERING AN INVASION 62
STUMBLING BLOCK .68
THE TIME IS 3AM 73
CONSIDER THIS 77
ALSO CONSIDER THIS 80
WHAT IF? 83
QUESTION ASKED .86
REVELATION 9:21 .89
THE GOSPEL 93

INTRODUCTION

If you have been a believer for any amount of years, you have probably heard many sermons. Sermons can be very uplifting, but can also become a replacement for personal study of the word. If the pastor only lives on other preacher's sermons and or books, then he passes on what the other preacher has heard from the other preacher . . . thus you end up with a misconstrued understanding of Scripture because of not taking it directly from the source yourself. This could very easily become unsound doctrine or even deception. Example: I'm sure you have heard the children's song, "This little light of mine, I'm gonna let it shine." Is this talking about a believer letting his light shine because the believer is a light or is it talking about that which a believer has received from God through revelation of His word, therefore, bringing light within the believer to shine? Through many sermons and worship sets, I've heard this put forth as a believer who is a light to the world. This has been passed down from generation to generation without studying it and taking to heart the context that it is in. This song was taken from Mark 4:21, *"Is a lamp brought to be put under a basket?"* When we read the verse just before this (4:20) it says those with good soil **hear** the word, accept it, and bear fruit. The verse following (4:22) says that nothing is hidden or in secret but that it should come to light. Then in conclusion Jesus says in verse 23-24

"If anyone has ears to hear, let him hear. Take heed what you hear. With the same measure you use (to search out the secret), *it will be measured to you; and to you who hear, more will be given."*

When a believer hears and accepts what he hears from God, a light comes on inside. God has an inexhaustible source of secrets that bring an inexhaustible light source within us, but there is one catch. What we put into obtaining these things is what we will receive. If you are a thirty-fold fruit bearer and desire to be a one hundred-fold fruit bearer, this can only happen because of the measure you use to receive it. So the light that is in us is the revelation of Jesus Christ that we have received. Notice verse 25 says whoever has, to him more will be given; **but** whoever does not have, even what he has will be taken away from him. If we rest on what we think we have, it could be taken away. I pray for an inexhaustible desire for God and the revelation of Jesus the Christ!

LIVING STONES
December 7, 2015

Jesus replied, *"If they keep quiet, the stones <u>along the road will burst into cheers</u>!"* (Luke 19:40 <u>LNT</u>)

I have heard preachers and songwriters say many times that if we don't praise Him, the rocks will shout out and praise Him. You get the picture from the verse above that the rocks along the road will begin to somehow start shouting "Praise the Lord" and "Blessed is He who comes in the name of the Lord" if we don't respond! Is this what Jesus meant when He said this? Was He putting ordinary rocks in competition with His people for praise? The translation above has indicated this through their interpretation of the verse. As we look into this Scripture and the context of this verse, we will begin to discover that what is proclaimed by Jesus is something completely different than what is being presented in this translation.

Let me first set the stage by going back a few chapters in Luke and see what Jesus was encountering and what was the set of

His heart. We'll begin at Luke 9:27-36 at the story of the Mount of Transfiguration; highlighting verses 30 and 31. It says that two men appeared and talked with Jesus while He was on the mountain. The two men, Moses and Elijah, spoke with Him concerning His death and departure from this world and that it would all be accomplished at Jerusalem! From this point on, everything surrounds His destiny to journey to Jerusalem. The very next day, coming down from the mountain, He encountered a situation of demonic possession and His disciples that couldn't get a child delivered from demons. His response to this is to be noted; *"How long shall I be with you and bear with you?"* (9:41) He knew that His time was short in regard to seeing faith established in His disciples, so He rebuked them for their unbelief. He then immediately says to them, *"Let these words sink down into your ears, for the Son of Man is about to be betrayed into the hands of men."* (9:44) His meeting with Moses and Elijah has confirmed His betrayal which in turn caused Jesus to set His face to go to Jerusalem as recorded in Luke 9:51; *"Now it came to pass, when the time had come for Him to be received up, that He steadfastly set His face to go to Jerusalem."* It was in Jerusalem that He would die and fulfill what God had revealed to Him through Moses and Elijah. This is now what is on Jesus' heart and mind through Chapter 9 leading up to the Triumphal Entry in Luke Chapter 19.

As His face was set towards Jerusalem, He could have had on His mind the Babylonian invasion and the destruction of the Temple resulting in the captivity of Jerusalem of which Isaiah, Jeremiah, and many other prophets spoke of. He could have been thinking about King David and his reign in Jerusalem of which was called Zion (the reign and dwelling place of God) the city of David. He could have been thinking about all the wickedness that went on in Jerusalem and the abominations that were set up in the Temple as is recorded in Ezekiel 8. Jesus was aware of the Father's heart towards Israel and Jerusalem of which is recorded throughout the prophets. He **is** the Father's heart manifested in flesh and blood! As He rode towards Jerusalem those who had been touched by His life were crying out with loud voices saying, *"Blessed is the King who comes in the name of the Lord!"* This greatly irritated the religious leaders who began yelling at Him from the crowd, *"Teacher rebuke Your disciples."*

This takes us back to our original Scripture where Jesus responds to the Pharisees concerning the stones crying out. Were the stones mentioned by Jesus just stones on the ground along side the road or did they represent something of greater magnitude? As we contemplate all that Jesus had gone through leading up to this point, we can't help but think that His heart is broken because of what has happened to the Temple and Jerusalem throughout history. All this happened because of the disobedience and the hardness of the heart of His people; and here He is experiencing this very same thing with the religious leaders. Luke mentions that as He was nearing Jerusalem, He began to weep over it saying, *"If you had known, even you, especially in this your day, the things that make for your peace!* He goes on to say that the days will come when her enemies will not leave one stone upon another; they will be thrown down! This will happen because she didn't know the time of her visitation (the coming of the Messiah). Mark brings out an important point that no other gospel writer had mentioned. He points out that when Jesus had come into Jerusalem He went into the Temple and looked around at all that was going on, but decided to go to Bethany to spend the night because it was already late. (Luke 11:11) Can you imagine what was in His heart as He looked around and saw all the people selling merchandise in His Father's house? The very next day in what seemed to be a very random act, He cursed a fig tree. This just happened to be on His way to the Temple in which He immediately entered and did what was on His heart the night before. He began to drive out those who were merchandizing; overturning their tables and not allowing anyone to carry merchandise through it. I believe He did this with a grieving heart! As we continue, you will see that Jesus again speaks of stones being thrown down. Following the cleansing of the Temple, we see Jesus teaching in the temple daily being encountered by the religious leaders who were trying to trap Him. It comes to the point were Jesus has to completely reveal their hypocrisy. In Matthew 23, Jesus pronounces seven woes against the scribes and Pharisees calling them hypocrites. He ends this dissertation of rebuke with a word against Jerusalem, but He addresses her as corporate Israel (the one who kills the prophets sent to her). He says to her, *"See! Your house is left to you desolate; for I say to you, you shall see Me no more till you say, 'Blessed is He who comes in the name of the Lord!'"* It is here that He tells His disciples that not one stone (of Jerusalem's house) will be left upon another, but they will all be thrown down. (Matthew 24:2) In the building of the Temple these stones were placed one upon another in the very presence and under the direction of God. Originally Solomon had built the Temple and each stone of the Temple was carefully placed in the loving fear of the Lord. The workmen were hand picked and were dedicated to perfection and holiness as they built the Temple. God put His signature on this Temple, when the Ark was brought into it, by filling it with the cloud of His presence so that the priests had to stop ministering because of the weight of the glory that had filled the house! (1Kings 8:10-11) God called it "My house!" *"For My house shall be called a house of prayer for all nations."* (Isaiah 56:7) Now as He was descending down the Mount of Olives on the donkey, the city of Jerusalem and the Temple were clearly seen. At this very time the Pharisees are rebuking Him because of what His followers were proclaiming concerning Him. They were proclaiming Him as *King*! His heart was moved for Jerusalem and her people. His Father's house was filled with wickedness and merchandizing. His response to the Pharisees came from deep within the heart of the Father and Jesus spoke it out. *"I tell you that if these should keep silent, the stones would immediately cry out."* (Luke19;40 NKJV) The very stones that built Jerusalem and the very stones that made up His Temple would cry out!

    Place yourself in the position of one of these stones. What would you have heard and seen on the streets of Jerusalem throughout the pages of history? If you were a stone in the wall of the Temple what would you have heard spoken day after day? What would you have seen in the Temple as you observed the priests carrying out their priestly duties before God? Solomon alone offered 120,000 sheep just at the dedication of the Temple. (2 Chronicles 7:5) How much blood would you have seen being spilled for the sins of each person individually? How many prophecies of the coming Messiah would you have heard day after day being proclaimed within the walls of the Temple? I would say that if you were a stone in the wall of Jerusalem, you would have heard Jeremiah prophesying of the coming destruction from Babylon because Israel had forsaken their God. You would have heard the voice of the false prophets saying that Jeremiah was speaking lies and that God would protect Israel in spite of this. You would have seen Jeremiah thrown down a well shaft and left for dead. Then you would have heard the warning trumpets sounding as Babylon came. You would hear the screams of women as their husbands and children were being slaughtered. You would have heard the sound of Babylonian horses and chariots trampling those in the streets. You would have heard the weeping of those who were being carried off to Babylon as captives to go to a strange and foreign city to live out their days as a slave. After all this you would hear the sound of silence and only the feeble footsteps of the poor who had been left in Jerusalem to live out their days in poverty. Where was their Deliverer that the stones in the walls had heard proclaimed so boldly day after day and year after year? The book of Isaiah was read within these walls and heard by every one of these stones. *"Behold, the virgin shall conceive and bear a Son, and shall call His name Immanuel* (God with us)*." "For unto us a Child is born, unto us a Son is given; and the government will be upon His shoulder. And His name will be called Wonderful, Counselor, Mighty God, Everlasting Father, Prince of Peace."* (Isaiah 7:14 and 9:6) I ask you, did Israel believe these words that Isaiah spoke? All of these things came upon Israel and Jerusalem because they didn't believe! They pursued other gods and their own selfish lives. All of these stones would have heard Jesus speak in the Temple regarding the fulfillment of Isaiah's prophecies. They saw every healing and miracle that Jesus had performed within her walls. These very stones heard the words of accusation and rejection from the Jews and religious leaders as they spewed out their anger and hatred upon the very Messiah that God had sent them. Yes, Jesus wept as He spoke these very words: *"O Jerusalem, Jerusalem, the one who kills the prophets and stones those who are sent to her. How often I wanted to gather your children together, as a hen gathers her chicks under her wings, but you were not willing! See! Your house is left to you desolate!" Then Jesus went out and departed from the Temple.* (Matthew23:37-24:1) I can hear the stones of the Temple crying out as Jesus leaves, "Wait! You are the Messiah! You are the One who is to come! Wait! You are the Holy One of Israel! You are our King! Yes, and Jesus would answer and say to us, I tell you that if you should keep silent, the stones would cry out!

THE SCOFFING SYNDROME
December 10, 2015

    If you have been a believer for twenty, thirty, or even forty years you have most likely had someone tell you, either in a sermon or by way of an article or book, that Jesus is coming back. They give their reasons as to why they believe this, of which much study and research has gone into. Then they do the unthinkable and tell you that He is coming back on April 1st. Yes, I know that this is April Fool's Day, but I had to add a little humor. The sad thing is that many people will listen to this and begin to prepare for His coming. I knew a married couple that received a prophetic word from a certain "respected" man of God. This man of God told his hearers to sell much of what they had and to prepare and wait for Jesus to come on the day that he had noted. This couple did exactly what this man told them to do. They sold much of what they had and sat in their house on that day waiting for Jesus to come for them. These people were not "nuts and flakes" as you suppose. They were sincere and loved God and desperately wanted Him to return. I remember that day because I lived a couple blocks away from them and I wondered as I passed their house what was going through their minds as they sat in their house waiting. I know what was going through my mind at that time. I was thinking, what if they are right and He does come? I wasn't being a total skeptic at the time, yet I thought it was a little presumptuous to think that God would reveal to someone the very day His Son would return to take us home. I later discovered in Scripture that even Jesus doesn't know the day or the hour that He Himself will return. Only the Father knows this day so how can we think He will reveal it to us when the Son doesn't even know? Here is the Scripture that says this: *"But of that day and hour no one knows, not even the angels in heaven, nor the Son, but only the Father."* (Mark13:32)

      This story is only one of many that I have encountered since I have become a believer. We live in days that are so filled with uncertainty and confusion. Jesus' return would be so welcomed! This is the reason that many hang on words like this one hoping that they are right. Within these unfulfilled stories that we encounter there is a simple principle in operation as we hear these predictions and then find out, with much disappointment, that they were false. The fable below brings out this principle. Remember Aesop's Fable of the little shepherd boy that cried wolf? He sat on the hillside watching the villager's sheep. He became bored and started crying out "Wolf! Wolf! A wolf is coming!" All the villagers ran as fast as they could up the hill to chase the wolf away, but found there was no wolf. They told the boy not to cry wolf when there was no wolf. He did this twice and on the third time the wolf came and the villagers didn't respond and the wolf had his way with the sheep. At sunset the villagers wondered why the boy had not brought the sheep to the village so they went up the hill to see what had happened only to find out that a wolf really had come. The boy felt very bad and one of the villagers comforted him yet said to him, "Nobody believes a liar, even when he is telling the truth!" The point of telling this story is to highlight something that isn't brought out within this story. The third time the boy cried wolf, the villagers didn't come running. They actually began mocking and scoffing the little boy's words! They didn't take into consideration that maybe there was a wolf, and so they became filled with skepticism. The result was disastrous!

If you're like me, you will find yourself skeptical when you encounter someone who is very zealous and adamant about the nearness of the Lord's return. Maybe they don't give a date, but still your response is to give into a little skepticism. "Yah, I know! I've heard that before!" This is not usually spoken, but carried within the secret place of your heart. You wouldn't dare say this out loud, but keep it as a secret in your heart. This is a scoffing heart! It is so subtle that we are not even aware of it. Jude brings out this very thing in his letter; *"Remember the words which were spoken before by the apostles of our Lord Jesus Christ: how they told you that there would be mockers in the last time . . .who cause divisions, not having the Spirit."* (verses 17-19) We must be careful that we do not carry the same kind of heart as these mentioned in Jude. Peter also warns us to watch over our hearts and not be caught up in this skepticism. *"Knowing this first: that scoffers will come in the last days, walking according to their own lusts, and saying, 'Where is the promise of His coming? For since the fathers fell asleep, all things continue as they were from the beginning of creation.' "* (1Peter3:3-4) Most of us read these verses with other people in mind and not ourselves. We remove ourselves thinking it's not talking about us, yet our thoughts accuse us of this very thing. If we were honest with ourselves, we would agree that there has come a certain amount of skepticism when we've faced disappointment after disappointment in regard to the Lord's return. Sometimes it just looks as if He has forgotten us and left us to fend for ourselves. I think this is why Jesus said when He returns, will He find faith on the earth? Our faith seems so weak at times; yet even in our weak faith, God knows our hearts and comes to encourage us. I love this about God. Even our weak yes makes Him excited.

    I would like to illustrate just a little bit further what scoffing actually looks like using one of Jesus' parables. *"Who then is a faithful and wise servant, whom his master made ruler over his household, to give them food in due season? Blessed is that servant whom his master, when he comes, will find so doing. Assuredly, I say to you that he will make him ruler over all his goods. But if that evil servant says in his heart, 'My master is delaying his coming', and begins to beat his fellow servants, and to eat and drink with the drunkards, the master of that servant will come on a day when he is not looking for him and at an hour that he is not aware of, and will cut him in two and appoint him his portion with the hypocrites."* (Matthew24:45-51) Again, we say, this does not refer to me, but to others. I would then ask, if we are wise servants, then why wouldn't we be willing to give the household of God their food in due season? If we see Jesus coming back soon, we will prepare God's household for this. If this is the season for the Lord's return, then we must get His household ready as John the Baptist did when he told the people to prepare the way of the Lord. Jesus said in another parable that we should let our waist be girded and our lamps burning; and be like men who wait for their master . . . and if he should come in the second watch or come in the third watch and find them so, blessed are those servants. Beloved how many watches have you gone through? We can either get happy or scoff. The will of the Father is to have faith and await Jesus' return. When we take the attitude that Jesus has been delayed and we don't treat our fellow servants with love and respect, then we have a scoffing heart that says Jesus isn't coming for awhile. Notice Jesus called this servant evil. A scoffing heart is evil! Paul prays for us because of this very thing: *"And this I pray, that your love may abound still more and more in knowledge and all discernment, that you may approve the things that are excellent, that you may be sincere and without offense till the day of Christ."* (Philippians 1:9-10) When we have a scoffing heart, we have allowed offense to come in. I remember a man named Harold Camping. Sound familiar? He predicted the return of Jesus on a specific day -- May 21, 2011; He didn't come on that day! He then said he had missed it and predicted another day -- October 21, 2011; it didn't happen that day either. I have heard more criticism of this man and yet he is a lot like us. He was awaiting the Lord's return, anticipating it very soon. Many became offended at his predictions and spoke very unkindly of him. I'm sure Jesus was happy to welcome him home when he passed, yet we judged him and said he was a flake. Which watch did Harold Camping proclaim? The 15th? The 20th? Were you ready, without offense, if Jesus were to have come on that day or did you scoff and become offended at his foolish prediction? Paul again exhorts us to watch and wait: *"And may the Lord make you increase and abound in love to one another and to all, just as we do to you, so that He may establish your hearts blameless in holiness before our God and Father at the coming of our Lord Jesus Christ with all His saints."* (1Thessalonians 3:12-13) I struggle with sarcasm and skepticism also. I am so quick to declare someone foolish and flaky. The end result of our faith has to be anticipating (on tiptoe) the return of Jesus Christ, because all throughout Scripture, Old and New Testament, it proclaims the coming of the Lord. The book of Isaiah alone has the phrase "in that day" several times throughout the book. You can't help but think that he is referring to the Lord's coming every time this statement is made. Look into it yourself. Don't just take my word for it. I must end with a question: As you have read this and observed the Scriptures that were presented, were you aware of your heart's attitude? If there was no excitement about Jesus' return could you be a scoffer?

THE IMAGE
December 11, 2015

To begin the unveiling of this mystery, I must start with Genesis 1:26-27, *"Then God said, 'Let Us make man in Our image, according to Our likeness . . .' So God created man in His own image; in the image of God He created him."* Before man was even created, God had an image of His own likeness. In the beginning His image was not something seen by the eye of man, but invisible. His own image was a very picture of Himself manifested within His very own being. This image was manifested within man at the creation. In Ezekiel Chapter 1, we see this image as described by Ezekiel in verses 26-28. Again, as we read this we must remember God created man in His own image and likeness. *"Above the firmament over their heads was the likeness of a throne, in appearance like a sapphire stone; on the likeness of the throne was a likeness with the appearance of a man high above it."* The Scripture goes on to describe what the image or the appearance of the man looked like, but the emphasis that I would like to make is on the likeness or image of God that he was seeing. We see Ezekiel's response to this vision at the end of verse 28, but what must be noted is that the likeness that he was seeing was speaking to him. Ezekiel said when he saw the vision, he fell on his face and heard a voice. The image or likeness of God was speaking directly to Ezekiel. Isaiah also had a vision of the likeness of God in chapter 6:1, *"In the year that King Uzziah died I saw the Lord sitting on a throne, high and lifted up, and the train of His robe filled the temple."* Isaiah not only saw the likeness of God on His throne, but he also saw the train of His robe filling the temple which represented His dominion and that all authority was given to Him to rule and reign in holiness and righteousness from His own temple. This was in stark contrast to Uzziah who became proud and entered the temple to burn incense. Because of his pride, while in the temple, he became leprous and was a leper until the day of his death. (2 Chronicles 26:16-21) In this we see the Lord's jealousy that He should be revered by man as holy. Again, it must be noted in Isaiah 6:8 that the likeness that Isaiah was observing was also speaking to him. *"Also I heard the voice of the Lord, saying. . . "* We must conclude that the Lord and His very image desire to speak to man who has been created in that image.

All this being said we will move on to the book of Revelation chapter 13 starting at verse 1, *"I saw a beast rising up out of the sea, having seven heads and ten horns, and on his horns ten crowns, and on his heads a blasphemous name. Now the beast which I saw was like a leopard, his feet were like the feet of a bear, and his mouth like the mouth of a lion. The dragon gave him his power, his throne, and great authority."* Comparing these words to what we just observed above in relation to God, we can't help but see that this beast has an image or likeness also as described in these verses. That being said, we must look at verses 5 and 6, *"He was given a mouth speaking great things and blasphemies, and he was given authority to continue for forty two months. Then he opened his mouth."* This beast and his image opened his mouth to speak! He was speaking in the hearing of his servants. What was he speaking? In verse 6, we see that he was speaking blasphemy against God; blaspheming His name, His tabernacle, and those who dwell in heaven. In other words, he was calling himself God and putting down to destroy everything that the true God represents. God the Father's tabernacle is the representation of His presence manifested to man in relationship with man. This beast wants to take God's place in heaven in order to draw all men to himself. In other words, he wants to de-throne God and set up his throne that all may worship him and hear his voice and obey him. What do we see in the earth at this very moment but the infiltration of Islam and Allah being the representation of God. The very desire of most of Allah's children is for his kingdom to reign throughout all of the earth. Revelation 13:8 actually says that all who dwell on the earth will worship him, whose names have not been written in the Book of Life of the Lamb slain from the foundation of the world. Our relationship with this Lamb is vitally important in order for us to overcome as this unfolds in the world.

    We also see another beast coming to the forefront in Revelation 13:11-15. He also has a description; two horns like a lamb and speaking like a dragon (looking humble, but speaking deceptive wickedness). He has a greater mission than himself in that he performs great signs to deceive and cause all to worship this first beast. What could this be but a false christ or messiah who points everyone to Allah. I believe he could be the Mahdi that the Koran speaks of. In verse 14 he tells people to make or create an image to the beast (Allah). In creating an image of Allah, this second beast must perform great signs in order to deceive the world. The image that has been created, because of great signs and wonders, is then given breath and the ability to speak. If you don't worship this beast's image you will be killed, for in his ability to speak he causes the killing of those who don't worship him. We see this happening today in Islam. So in light of what these Scriptures say, will we see men bow before a created idol (graven image) or will they bow before an unseen image which has been created through lying signs and wonders? Please understand, he has the number of a man (verse 18). Not as God who is and was and will always be (eternal), but numbers have an end because the number is named (666) the number of a (man). If a child says he can count to 1,000,000,000,000,000+ but in reality only makes it to 666, you have just seen the end of his counting ability. Daniel addressed King Belshazzar and the writing on the wall as he began to interpret the words: *"Mene: God has numbered your kingdom, and finished it."* I hope you get this. God has an image and He created man in that image. Also the first beast of Revelation 13 has an image and it's because of the second beast performing great wonders to deceive people into giving this beast his image with the ability to speak (verse 14). God's image is by God and speaking with God (example: "Let Us make man"). The beast's image is made by man through Satan's power and speaking to man (example: "Let us make a god"). Paul describes this beast in 2 Thessalonians 2:3-4,9-12. *"The son of perdition (doom AMP) who opposes and exalts himself above all that is called God or that is worshiped, so that he sits as God in the temple of God, showing himself that he is God." "The coming lawless one is according to the working of Satan, with all power, signs and lying wonders, and with all unrighteous deception among those who perish, because they did not receive the love of the truth, that they might be saved. And for this reason God will send them strong delusion, that they should believe the lie* (that he is God), *that they all may be condemned who did not believe the truth but had pleasure in unrighteousness."* Paul is saying the image of this man has been exalted because of lying wonders from Satan who has deceived those who have rejected the truth and became full of delusion. They enjoyed the pleasures of living in sinfulness and so it happened!

Simplified: God has an image that He created man in. Since the fall God has consistently made His image known to man in Scripture, ultimately resulting in Jesus Christ who is in the exact image of God. Since the fall, Satan also has endeavored to make himself an image to be believable by man, which is recorded throughout Scripture and will ultimately result in the man of sin displaying miraculous signs, establishing an image to the beast that man will worship, and man hearing that image speak to him. This image will be proclaimed as eternal, indestructible, intolerable, and to be God himself. I believe Allah and his messiah to come fits this description.

HE'S LOOKING FOR FRUIT
December 17, 2015

"He who abides in Me, and I in him, bears much fruit; for without Me you can do nothing." (John 15:5)

    For many years I have struggled to understand this saying of Jesus. It has put me through many agonizing days of wondering if I had fruit in my life. I didn't see much fruit in my life according to Galatians 5:22. I did see love, but not much joy or peace and my longsuffering was more like waiting for the person to fall so they wouldn't be a thorn anymore. Self-control was out the window and I took great pride in my faithfulness - when I was. I was not a gentle person, so no fruit in that area. I found myself in a real dilemma! Then for a period of time in my life I thought winning souls was to be my fruit. It works when your winning souls, but not so much if you're not. You start to wonder if you are really connected with the Vine. From this point I found myself in a desperate situation so I began saying yes to every event and ministry that the church had to offer; evangelism, music, discipleship, prison work, drama, artwork, leadership, service, etc., etc., etc. Oh yah, I'm going to bring forth some fruit now I thought. I found myself exhausted and burnt out. Learning to say no is a very important part of bearing fruit.

In the book of Isaiah it is brought out that God is looking for good fruit. *"Now let me sing to my Well-beloved a song of my Beloved regarding His vineyard: My Well-beloved has a vineyard on a very fruitful hill . . . He expected it to bring forth good grapes, but it brought forth wild grapes . . . What more could have been done to My vineyard?"* (Isaiah 5:1-4) We see in Isaiah the emphasis on the vineyard, but there is also emphasis on the fruit of it. Everything was perfect in the vineyard except for having good grapes. God is looking for the sweet fruit that it might be enjoyed. He's not looking to make a profit off of the grapes; He's looking for sweet fruit. Jesus makes this point in two parables that are addressed to the religious leaders; both being in Matthew 21:28-41: There was a man who had two sons and he asked them to work in the vineyard. One said that he wouldn't, but then did anyway. The other son said that he would, but then went his own way. After Jesus spoke the parable, He asked the religious leaders which one had done the will of his father? They answered the first son. Jesus' response is most revealing: *"Assuredly, I say to you that tax collectors and harlots enter the kingdom of God before you."* In other words they are willing to work in the vineyard to bring forth the sweet fruit (the kingdom of God). The other parable: A landowner created a vineyard with all the necessary ingredients to bring forth sweet fruit. At vintage time he sent servants to receive the sweet fruit but the (religious) vinedressers beat, stoned, and killed them. Then he sent his son, and they threw him out of the vineyard and killed him. Jesus' response: *"He will destroy those wicked men miserably, and lease his vineyard to other vinedressers who will render to him the* (sweet) *fruits in their seasons."* Again, God is looking for sweet fruit! He is not looking for our works or what we can do for Him in building His kingdom. Nor is He looking for perfect character or obedience (although very important). There is a factor that seems to get overlooked many times in our search to bring forth fruit. It's called *relationship*! Notice back in John 15:2; Jesus says that every branch that doesn't bear fruit He takes away or cuts it off. The branches that bear fruit will receive His very personal care by cutting off (pruning back) everything that doesn't have anything to do with Him baring fruit. He's looking for more sweet fruit. The more He can get, the more blessed He is. The key word in this is "abide." Abiding is an intimate, relational word. When you abide with someone, you have desire to be constantly with them. This is brought out in Jesus' response to His disciples at the last supper. He took the cup giving thanks and gave it to them saying to drink from it, because it was His blood shed for forgiveness of sins. Then He makes this statement: *"But I say to you, I will not drink of this fruit of the vine from now on until that day when I drink it new with you in My Father's kingdom."* (Matthew 26:29) Was Jesus talking about the cup that they had just shared or something else? In seeing God's desire for a fruitful vineyard in which He has sweet fellowship with those who love Him, we cannot help but see that Jesus is just like His Father. He looks forward to and longs greatly for the intimate fellowship with His disciples. He has already told them that He was going away after His death and resurrection. But the desire of His heart is to experience forever the sweet fruit of their fellowship. John 15 speaks of abiding and bringing forth this sweet fruit. John 16 speaks of the Holy Spirit guarding, protecting, comforting, and revealing Jesus to them while He's gone. Also, John 17 speaks of His prayer for them while He is gone. He prays in verse 15 for them to be kept from the evil one. Then He reveals His very heart again in verse 24 as He prays, *"Father, I desire that they also whom You gave Me may be with Me where I am, that they may behold My glory."* His strong desire is for us to be with Him in sweet fellowship! This vineyard is again described in detail in Revelation 21 and 22; only the description of it is very different.

THE MOST MISINTERPRETED SCRIPTURE EVER

December 18, 2015

"Who is worthy to open the scroll and to loose its seals?" Revelation 5:2

Plain and simple the emphasis is on the scroll and not the seals. Verse 3 mentions that no one in all of heaven and earth and even under the earth was able to open the scroll, or to even look at it; and verse 4 speaks of John weeping over that fact. The scroll was the main focus of attention by the One who sat on the throne, by the angel crying "who is worthy", by John who was weeping, and by the elder who responded to John. The elder emphasized the priority of the scroll first and then the seals. In verse 7, we see a picture of confidence, holiness, and relationship between Father and Son.
"Then He came and took the scroll out of the right hand of Him who sat on the throne." Jesus was saying as He walked up to His Father, "I'll take that scroll and open it!" But there was a slight problem; the

scroll had seals on it so it couldn't be opened. The first four seals are judgments that have been released on the earth throughout history from the beginning. The fifth seal are martyrs (who had been killed by people like Cain, Saul, Ahab and Jezebel and the like throughout the history of the earth) seeking closure. The sixth seal is all the rulers of the earth and those that followed them dominating the earth with ungodly ideologies and dictating them to those of the earth. The seventh seal are fallen angels and Satan orchestrating his plan to dominate the earth and man through destruction on the earth and the manifestation of his evil purposes through a flesh and blood messiah (the anti-christ beast). Yes, these are devastating to earth and man; **but**, in the end these seven seals must be broken off of the scroll for it to be looked at and read! They are not released by Jesus as He opens them; **they are being brought to nothing!** As He opens them they are being put under His feet! The power of these seven seals has finally been stopped forever because He was the only one found worthy to do this! Now is the time to have a Hallelujah breakdown!!

THE STUPID ROOM
December 16, 2015

    Cory Russell, who is a leader and teacher at IHOP-KC, gave a message at a Onething Conference directed at the young people gathered. He commended them for their desire for God and for seeking God with all of their hearts, but then mentioned the tendency for young people to stay up very late into the night. He indicated that this staying up late usually caused most teenagers to enter the "stupid room." He was meaning that they do things that are completely against desiring and seeking God during those late night hours. The night then ends with shame and numbness that makes it a tremendous struggle to get back to the place of intimacy with Jesus. He was exhorting thousands of young people to stay out of the "stupid room!"

    Unfortunately it's not just young people that enter the "stupid room." And, there are many other ways than staying up late that can bring one into this room. I was in my 30's and still went into this room very often. I will explain. Living in a Christian community was a tremendous blessing. Over the course of the 20 years that I was in that community, I had grown in the Lord and became a changed man, but there were still areas that showed tremendous weakness. I was somewhat of a jokester and loved to do things that would irritate my brothers and sisters. Sometimes things would be funny and other times it would backfire -- real bad! All this said, I would find myself in the stupid room just because I tried to make people laugh. I would do things like grab someone's socks and stretch them a bit and then tie them together so they couldn't walk. Some people would roll with this and others would be real upset. Wrestling was a favorite pass time among the brothers and yet would often end up with someone getting hurt. I could have spent time seeking the Lord, but instead would enter the stupid room. There are so many other things that could be shared (some very personal), but I think you get the point. Below I have compiled a list of what I think are legitimate situations that describe entering the "Stupid Room!" This list is not exhaustive so please feel free to add to it. Hope you like them.

If you consider yourself a believer in Jesus, then you'll find yourself in the stupid room if you:

- Choose to watch TV for 4 hours and then have no time to spend with God in prayer.
- Very seldom read your Bible.
- Listen to Rock and Roll or any secular music artist and drink from that well continuously.
- Speak one way around believers, but cuss and swear around non-believers.
- Play video games into the wee hours of the morning.
- Play video games over and over in order to beat the game no matter how long it takes.
- Decide that wine is the alternative for water at every meal.
- Drink wine or beer to get a buzz.
- Have a "brew and bible study" in the local pub.
- Watch football or basketball from Saturday afternoon through Sunday evening every weekend.

- Sit in Church and worry that the service will go to long so that you will miss part of the game.
- Are a pastor of a church and participate in one of the above.
- Are at a family gathering and on your cell phone just like everyone else.
- Stay up all night doing "<u>dumb things</u>" and then sleep all day.
- Go on shopping binges just to get the latest fashions.
- Smoke cigarettes, E-cigs, or cigars.
- Find someone's wallet full of money with their name and address in it, but decide to take the money.
- Click on that questionable website just out of curiosity.
- Have to win every argument with your spouse.
- Side with an issue knowing that it is an abomination in the sight of God.
- Pursue someone of the opposite sex while married to your spouse.
- Think your kids are not watching you when you do what you do.
- Go on uncontrollable eating binges.
- Act and dress like you're a teenager thinking it is cool.

THE HELPER
December 23, 2015

"And the Lord God said, 'It is not good that man should be alone; I will make him a helper comparable to him.'" *"For Adam there was not found a helper comparable to him. And the Lord God caused a deep sleep to fall on Adam, and he slept, and He took one of his ribs, and closed up the flesh in its place. Then the rib which the Lord God had taken from man He made into a woman, and He brought her to the man."* (Genesis 2:18-22)

God created a helper for man that would be bone of his bone and flesh of his flesh; someone that would come along side of man and be a comfort, support, and also bring much affirmation to his life. We know from Scripture that Adam's helper didn't help him much when confronted by the serpent, but led him into sin of which he willingly participated. The helper became a hindrance. I don't say this to put women in a position of being on the defense, but to simply present that God wanted a helper for man. Because of the fall, this position has been extremely tainted to the point of rampant divorce and the break up of families. Many children have been raised without the godly influence of a father in the home. I see this vacancy in young men who then can't find out who they are and who God created them to be; they keep searching for an example. The examples of godly men are way to few to go around for those young men that need one. So they are left to discover their own examples of what a father is from Hollywood, the music industry, and any man that has an influence. Young women are left searching for this same example, however, in the process they become men haters, yet still searching for a man to meet their needs. In their search they don't really trust men, so the relationship is doomed to fail even before it starts. What I am about to present is what I believe to be God's perfect answer to this dilemma. Before I expound on this, I re-emphasize that man needs a helper suitable to bring him into all he was created to be. When I use the term "man" I use the term generically. Man was created in the image of God. Woman was created in the likeness of man with God's image upon her as well. When the phrase "bone of my bone and flesh of my flesh" is used, it describes the oneness and mutual helping of each other. There is a major breakdown of this in marriages today. What is the answer? Another Helper! This Helper will introduce us to the Father. When Jesus speaks of His God, He uses the term "Father." This is recorded a total of twenty-two times in John chapter 14 alone, and another thirty-five times in chapters 15-17. He is endeavoring to communicate something extremely important in this discourse to His disciples.

Jesus brings home the fact that man needs a father figure in his life. Misty Edwards has a line in one of her songs that says "broken fathers make broken children." We need a perfect Father to undue our brokenness! In John Chapter 14, we see phrases like these:

- In My **Father's** house . . .
- No one comes to the **Father** except through Me.
- If you had known Me, you would have known My **Father**.
- He who has seen Me has seen the **Father**.

- Do you not believe that I am in the **Father**, and the **Father** in Me?
- Believe Me that I am in the **Father** and the **Father** in Me.
- Greater works than these he will do, because I go to My **Father**.
- Whatever you ask in My name, that I will do, that the **Father** may be glorified in the Son.

I must make a statement at this time in regard to the "greater works" message that seems so prevalent in the pulpit today. Jesus is making a statement about our relationship with the Father and how important it is, yet we have taken out of the heart of this message the "greater works" statement and made it the main message. Signs, wonders, and miracles are to follow believers, but we are not to make this the main emphasis. Jesus said that a wicked generation seeks after a sign, yet when signs are given they still refuse to believe.

When Jesus makes these statements about the Father, it is then that He presents the answer to the dilemma of our brokenness. *"If you love Me, keep My commandments. And I will pray the **Father**, and He will give you **another Helper**."* (John 14:15-16 – emphasis mine) This Helper will be with you forever! (verse 16) This Helper is unseen by the rest of the world. This Helper is also called the Spirit of Truth and you will know Him because He will live in you! He's not just called along side to help, He takes up residence within the very one who needs the Helper. The Helper is the direct representation of the Father as John 14:26 says, *"The Helper, the Holy Spirit, whom the **Father** will send."* (emphasis mine) The Father sends the direct representation of Himself through Jesus to us. Yes, Jesus is also the representation of the Father, but He could not stay with us as He tells us in John 16:7 which says, *"It is to your advantage that I go away; for if I do not go away, the Helper will not come to you."* Our Helper has come to replace Jesus until He comes back. The Helper will convict of sin (the loving revelation that comes to us when we slip, trip, stumble, and fall.) The Helper will also convict of righteousness just as Jesus had done when He walked this earth. Jesus said He had to go to the Father and would not be seen on this earth anymore. His very presence manifested to us through the Helper proclaims within us that we are righteous before God! The Helper would also convict of judgment (if we give into and follow the ruler of this world) because he has been judged already.

Jesus gave us "another" Helper because He knew that not all would receive the benefits of the first helper. Unwanted singleness, divorce, unfaithfulness, and loneliness are a modern day plague. This Helper will never leave us, never forsake us, never badmouth us, never betray us, never speak badly about us, or ever run off with another lover. This Helper will be with us forever! He will not speak on His own authority, but whatever He hears He will speak (John 16:13). He speaks to reveal Jesus who is the exact representation of the Father! We are to be in intimate relationship with Jesus through the Holy Spirit. This is why Paul exhorts us to be filled with the Spirit in Ephesians 5:18. After he says this he expounds about the relationship between husbands and wives and how they are to behave towards one another. He quotes Genesis 2:24, which speaks about man being joined to his wife in one flesh of which he says is a great mystery. But what Paul is referring to is Christ Jesus in intimate relationship and oneness with the church. We are married to Him! The Helper brings us into what Revelation 19:7 proclaims; *"The marriage of the Lamb has come, and His wife has made herself ready."* Are you ready? Are you letting the Helper reveal and make you into His city? This is a revelation, not only of His death and resurrection, but of His exaltation and glorification: "The Lamb is the city's temple. The city had no need of the sun or moon to shine in it . . . the Lamb is its light." (Revelation 21:22-23)

Jesus also mentions something about the Helper that is extremely important and worth noting. Leading up to this statement, He mentions that He still had many things that He wanted to say to His disciples, but they just couldn't bear them at that time. He had told them He was leaving them and they were extremely sorrowful because of it. In other words, the things that He wanted to tell them would be clouded by their sorrow and would not be understood. These things were important so He says this to them: *"However, when He* (The Helper), *the Spirit of truth, has come, He will guide*

you into all truth; for He will not speak on His own authority, but whatever He hears He will speak; and He will tell you things to come." Jesus wanted to tell them about the future and what it would hold. He knew that it was important to let them (and us) know of these things so He mentions that the Helper will expound them to us. You will notice in Revelation 1:10 that John says he was in the Spirit on the Lord's Day. In other words, he was being helped by "The Helper" (the Holy Spirit) and he saw revelations! He saw Jesus glorified and fell as a dead man! He saw the last days played out before his very eyes! Remember Revelation 1:1 says, *"The Revelation of Jesus Christ, which God* (The Father) *gave Him to show His servants -- things which must shortly take place."*
Beloved, it's the revelation of Jesus Christ; not the last days! We must see this revelation! Many speak about the fact that this book is incomprehensible, yet rejoice because we know how it ends. True, but not comforting. Jesus speaks of the Father in John 14 as we have seen, but He also speaks of the Father in John 17:11-12; *"Now I am no longer in the world, but these are in the world, and I come to You Holy Father, keep through Your name those whom You have given Me."* What was His name that would keep us? Father! The fact that He is Holy and we can call Him Father is what will keep us through the last days as they unfold. Now is the time for a Holy Ghost breakdown!

THE LION
December 28, 2015

"Your adversary the devil walks about like a roaring lion, seeking whom he may devour." 1 Peter 5:8

Most would say of this lion that he is a destroyer and seeks to kill and devour. Most would also say that the lion that they serve; The Lion of Judah; is my protector and my deliverer; the one whom I follow!" This is true concerning Jesus, but regarding the characteristics of a lion, this would be comparable to Aslan from Narnia. But in real life, if you were to come face to face with a lion, there would come great fear and dread. You will see in the next few paragraphs that the characteristics of these two lions described in 1 Peter 5:8 and Revelation 5:5 are very similar. There is only one difference that must be pointed out: Peter says the devil is "like" a lion; so not really being a lion; but what would be our conclusion concerning the Lion of Judah?

Before I get into this I would like to share a story about my wife and I and our experience before marriage. We both lived in a Christian community which had some very strict rules about relationships and dating. This community was birthed in 1972 during the Jesus Movement. Because of the immorality that was rampant coming out of the hippie generation, the community put these rules into place for our protection. If a man on staff desired to develop a deeper relationship with a woman on staff, he had to first clear it through the pastor and the leadership of the community. Then, when the okay was given, he could pursue a dating relationship with her. The only catch was that the man couldn't express how he felt about the woman until his request was cleared by leadership. Sandy and I both had experienced broken marriages before we came to the Lord. This seemed to be a point of hesitancy in the pastor. We both knew what it was like to experience divorce and all the baggage that goes with it. We not only had to carry this baggage, but we each had a child from these broken marriages. We both, however, still had a desire for marriage and to share our lives with someone. There was a void in our hearts which meant that we were not satisfied with singleness. The community we were involved with was extremely evangelistic. It was a common practice to be active in some kind of evangelism daily. We were given assignments and paired up with someone for these daily evangelism activities. Sandy and I would often get paired up as a team. Well, you can guess what happened. We had such a great time together that we started having feelings for each other. I found myself talking to her one day and let my feelings out (just a little). That was all it took. I requested clearance from the pastor and leadership to go forward in a relationship. It was denied with the question; "How do you even know if you are eligible for re-marriage?" I was devastated. I went back to the pastor a few weeks later to present the same request. It was then told to me that both of us had to do a study on divorce and re-marriage and turn it in. I was diligent in this and discovered that both Sandy and I were eligible. I then turned in my study and waited for a response. And waited and waited and waited! I even turned in another note requesting this again. I waited and waited and waited! I must express the dynamics that I lived under and experienced while in this community. (Note: I have dealt with resentment and bitterness and hold no ill feelings toward anyone in regards to these things that I'm sharing.) The dynamics of the community were somewhat intimidating. If the pastor felt a check concerning anything negative in your life it was usually expressed in front of other staff members. If it was expressed, you then came under the disciplining hand of the Lord. Sometimes what you felt was from God was questioned and even rejected. For this reason, I waited instead of pressing it through. I didn't want to be labeled a rebel or unteachable by pushing too hard and then having the leadership reject it. I kept hoping that I would hear good news, but it didn't come in the time frame that I was expecting. I turned in my first note to the pastor and leadership on September 12, 1986. After approaching the pastor one more time and requesting an answer, the okay finally came. Date fulfilled --- September 15, 1987. One year later! We had both endured a year of silence; from leadership and toward each other because we couldn't even talk to each other except for casual conversation. Please understand the situation: The Church had an office in which Sandy was secretary and I was involved with maintenance of several apartments that the Church owned. This caused me to enter the office very regularly several times a day. Our exchange was "hi" and "bye". Do you know how hard that is??? There were times of correction because it was perceived that we had been spending to much time together in "casual talk." At the most we spent 15 minutes or less. Some of these corrections seemed to be very devastating to Sandy and I thought she would think the waiting and restrictions were too hard and would end up leaving staff. I was ready to walk out myself, but knew that God was in the waiting and the suffering of this thing. I was hoping Sandy believed the same. As I said, it was in September, 1987, that we began our life's journey towards marriage. Before the day we talked, I went out and bought a framed picture of two lions. The picture was a male and a female laying side by side. We had just come through the most enduring time of our life. We had conquered and devoured every obstacle in our way that year, along with putting to death every lie that screamed in our heads. This picture is still hanging in our house to this day. The Lion of Judah had caused us to overcome. You can see that back in 1987, before I even knew there was a Narnia, we had an Aslan who helped us come through every situation. Even after all these years I'm just now beginning to see Jesus, not as a Narnia type of lion, but as a devourer described within the following paragraphs.

The title and description of Jesus most used is taken from the book of Revelation chapter 5 verse 5, *"Behold the Lion of the tribe of Judah . . . has prevailed to open the scroll."* Since we see Jesus in Scripture as meek and lowly, forgiving and merciful, we know that He is like a lamb and so we receive from Him as a lamb. We assume that since the book of Revelation describes Him as a Lion that He will claim this title in the last of days and be bold and ruthless against His enemies. Yes, He will, but we are missing something very important that must be pointed out.

Beginning in Genesis 49:9 we see Jacob's prophecy over his son Judah: *"Judah, you are the one whom your brothers shall praise; your hand shall be on the neck of your enemies; your father's sons shall bow down to you.* **Judah, a lion's cub with the prey, my son, you have gone high up [the mountain]. He stooped down, he crouched like a lion, and like a lioness--who dares provoke and rouse him?"** (AMP - emphasis mine) His father, Jacob, is describing Judah as a lion. Not just any lion, but a lion that has caught his prey and doesn't want to share it. He is described as fearless, aggressive, and will not be provoked. As described above, we see the characteristics of Jesus as the Lion who comes from the tribe of Judah within many Bible characters. As we proceed through Scripture, we encounter Caleb, who is of the Tribe of Judah. God told Israel that they would possess the land of Canaan and it would be their land forever. You will recall that Caleb was one of the ten spies sent out by Moses to survey Canaan and bring back a report. When they returned, the other nine brought back a bad report. They saw giants and feared for their lives! But Caleb had a different spirit and told the people that they should go and possess it immediately because they were well able to take it. Caleb had the heart of a lion in fearlessness and courage because he believed God. As you recall, Caleb was one of only two of his generation that entered the promised land forty years later. The rest died in the wilderness. In looking at Joshua 14 we see Caleb's response to Joshua as he possesses his inheritance: *"You know the word which the Lord said to Moses the man of God concerning you and me . . . to spy out the land . . . Nevertheless my brethren who went up with me made the* *heart of the people melt, but I wholly followed the Lord my God. And now, behold, the Lord has kept me alive, as He said, these forty-five years . . . and now, here I am this day, eighty-five years old.* ***As yet I am as strong this day as on the day that Moses sent me . . . Now therefore, give me this mountain!"*** (emphasis mine) Caleb had an attitude of devouring just like a lion. He knew his God and believed all that He said. The Lion of the Tribe of Judah lived in Caleb. We see in Joshua Chapter 15 all the territory that the tribe of Judah conquered and possessed in the land of Canaan. Caleb had as his inheritance the city of Hebron, which had previously been occupied by Anakim; the giants who scared the other ten spies to death. The Lion of the Tribe of Judah was with Caleb as they marched across Canaan to possess it. Yet in all of their accomplishments, they failed to possess the city of Jebus which was occupied by the Jebusites (Genesis 15:63). This city was a stronghold for evil and the Jebusites wouldn't give it up, occupying it for several years until someone else from the tribe of Judah came along.

    David, the son of Jesse, was a young boy, who lived in Bethlehem, which was a city of Judah. He would look after his father's sheep and on occasion would be encountered by a lion that would attack the sheep. This didn't go well for the lion because the Lion of the Tribe of Judah was in David even in his young age. David recalls the encounter as he speaks to King Saul: *"Your servant used to keep his father's sheep, and when a lion or a bear came and took a lamb out of the flock, I went out after it and struck it, and delivered the lamb from its mouth; and **when it arose against me, I caught it by its beard, and struck and killed it."*** (1 Samuel 17:34-35 - emphasis mine) Is this not the Lion of the Tribe of Judah possessing one of His servants and accomplishing something that would be humanly impossible? David is giving his credentials to Saul for the sole purpose of encountering and killing the giant, Goliath. Yes David went on to kill Goliath with a sling and a stone, but what happened afterward is of great significance. After cutting off Goliath's head, the army of the children of Israel shouted and pursued the army of the Philistines and then returned to plunder their tents. David didn't go with them. David did something else that would change the course of history forever. You see when David cut off Goliath's head, he had something on his mind; unfinished business! While the armies of Israel and Judah attacked the Philistines, David took Goliath's head and carried it to Jerusalem. (1 Samuel 17:54) He was remembering the days when Israel invaded Canaan and the fact that Caleb and the tribe of Judah had not conquered and occupied Jebus (Jerusalem). We must understand that Jerusalem was not called by that name yet. David had not yet become king and Jerusalem was still called Jebus occupied by the Jebusites. (1 Chronicles 11:4) We know that David didn't immediately become king when Samuel anointed him. He went through many long years of running from Saul and then after Saul's death only reigned over the tribe of Judah for seven and a half years because of war between the house of Saul and the house of David. It wasn't till after all these years that the tribes of Israel desired to make David king. It was at this time that David fulfilled the prophetic act that he had made with Goliath's head. In taking his head to this city he was prophesying to the Jebusites that their time was coming! The Jebusites were emboldened into thinking the city of Jebus was an impenetrable city because the children of Judah didn't conquer it and many years had passed since Goliath's head was dropped off there. I can just imagine the bold arrogance being replaced by the fear of the Lord as they observed King David's rule becoming stronger. Within David lived the Lion of Judah! In fact the Lion of Judah was called the root of David in Revelation 5:5. David received his courage, and his attitude of devouring from his root (The Lion) the devourer!

We see this very thing in the Lord Himself as He addresses Ephraim and Judah in their sin: *"I will be like a lion to Ephraim, and like a young lion to the house of Judah. I, even I, will tear them and go away; I will take them away, and no one shall rescue. I will return again to My place till they acknowledge their offense. Then they will seek My face; in their affliction they will earnestly seek Me"* (Hosea 5;14-15). After what God had done to them He endeavors to call them to repentance saying: *"Come and let us return to the Lord; for **He has torn, but He will heal us**; He has stricken, but He will bind us up. After two days He will revive us; on the third day He will raise us up, that we may live in His sight."* (Hosea 6:1-2 - emphasis mine) God doesn't rip and tear us in order to destroy us even though it feels like it. He tears us in order to heal us rightly. We are broken and need to be torn so we can be healed in the right way. How does He heal us? By what He said in verse 2; as Jesus was raised on the third day, so He will heal us in raising us up also! So in the light of what the Scripture just said, we must be willing for God to consume and devour us into His very being. *"Who among us shall dwell with the devouring fire?"* (Isaiah 33:14) He is called the Lion of the Tribe of Judah because He is a devourer. He will not relent till He has it all. We also see this in Zephaniah 1:1-3, *"The word of the Lord which came to Zephaniah. . . **'I will utterly consume** everything from the face of the land,' says the Lord; **'I will consume** man and beast; **I will consume** the birds of the heavens, the fish of the sea, and all stumbling blocks along with the wicked.* (emphasis mine) What better way to die than to be consumed by the Lion of the Tribe of Judah! It's no wonder our adversary walks around like a roaring lion seeking to devour. His roar of deception is to bring us to the place of bondage and false worship. He is a counterfeiter! He desires to devour us so that he can have us as his prize! Joel 3:16 says, *"The Lord will also roar from Zion, and utter His voice from Jerusalem; The heavens and earth will shake; but the Lord will be a shelter for His people."* Even in the midst of a tremendous shaking coming in the earth caused by His roar, we will find shelter in His shadow. Yes, His roar will cause the shaking. He is coming to devour! He is coming with intense love to devour His people into His kingdom forever and He is coming to devour His enemies and destroy them forever.

YOU DO NOT KNOW WHAT YOU ASK
January 6, 2016

James and John came up to Jesus and asked Him if they could sit on His right and left hand with Him in His glory. (Mark 10:37) In other words they were asking to rule and reign with Him over the kingdom. How could they be so bold in asking Him this? The other ten knew they were dysfunctional fishermen and were no different than anyone else. So what prompted this request? We must look back at a moment in the lives of James and John in order to understand what lead up to this. Back in Mark 9:1, Jesus points out to those around Him saying that there were some standing among them that would not see death till they saw the kingdom of God with power. Six days later Peter, James, and John are on a mountain with Jesus and He becomes transfigured before their very eyes. He allows them to see Himself in His eternal state; brilliantly white -- the brightest that they had ever seen. This encounter ended with a voice from a cloud saying, *"This is My beloved Son. Hear Him!"* Father God had just established in James and Johns mind the rule and reign of His Son over everything and everyone everywhere.

Peter, James, and John being the only ones there to see this and then Jesus commanding them not to tell anyone, meant that it was to be a special secret between them. They felt that they now had an extra special relationship with Jesus. This is what happens to us when God reveals Himself through a vision or a revelation and we are affirmed by Him. We are just like James and John, thinking we have a special audience with Him and that we are deemed more important in His eyes because of it. We don't ask to sit on His right hand, but we ask to be raised up to a prominent place of influence. We ask to be well liked by everyone because we love Jesus. We seek for position that we would be looked up to by others. This is not a result of the fall nor is it sinful, but is the very nature and likeness of God within us. God Himself wants a prominent place of influence, to be liked and loved. His desire is for our good! If this desire in us for prominence is from God, then why did Jesus say to James and John, *"You do not know what you ask."* Does God have qualifications for positions?

Jesus follows His daunting statement with a question, *"Are you able to drink the cup that I drink, and be baptized with the baptism that I am baptized with?"* I have often found myself asking God about this question. What is this cup that we are to drink from? Is it at the communion table that we drink from it? In my own ignorance, I would say I was baptized in water just like Jesus was, so that should make me qualified to rule with Him. However, Jesus goes on to speak about being a servant and that whoever desires to be prominent in the kingdom must be a slave of all. Jesus, who could have ruled on this earth from the beginning, chose to be a servant and to give His life as a ransom. Webster defines ransom: a consideration paid or demanded for the release of someone from captivity. Isaiah expounds on this in chapter 53:

- *"He was wounded for our transgressions, He was bruised for our iniquities; the chastisement for our peace was upon Him, and by His stripes we are healed."*
- *"The Lord has laid on Him the iniquity of us all."*
- *"He was led as a lamb to the slaughter."*
- *"For the transgressions of My people He was stricken."*

- "It pleased the Lord to bruise Him; He has put Him to grief. When You make His soul an offering for sin, He shall see His seed."
- "By His knowledge My righteous Servant shall justify many, for He shall bear their iniquities."
- "He bore the sin of many, and made intercession for the transgressors." Isaiah 53:5-8, 10-12

I believe this is part of Jesus' baptism, yet how can we be baptized with His baptism in these things? Only Jesus can bear sin and iniquity. And what is the cup that He drinks? Jesus sees this cup as a dreadful thing because when He's in the garden He asks the Father to take it away, yet He also tells James and John that they can drink of it. I believe this cup is directly related to His sufferings. Paul tells the Philippians it has been granted on behalf of Christ to suffer for His sake. Paul also makes the statement that he might know Christ and the power of His resurrection, and the fellowship of His sufferings. (Philippians 1:29, 3:10) Jesus was asking James and John if they would suffer with Him by drinking from His cup. They were saying yes, we will. Did they really know what they were saying when they answered Him? Paul says in Romans 8:17 that we are heirs of God and joint heirs with Christ, but he qualifies this by saying we must suffer with Him. We will be glorified according to the amount of suffering we embrace. This is why Jesus asked if they were able to drink the cup. He knew it would be a difficult thing for them because He later told them that they were all going to stumble because of Him. Nobody wants to suffer especially for someone else.

Here are some verses from Isaiah 53 that parallel along with Jesus' baptism mentioned above. These verses deal with suffering and could be cause for us to fellowship in His sufferings:

- "He is despised and rejected by men, a man of sorrows and acquainted with grief."
- "He was despised, and we did not esteem Him."
- "We esteemed Him stricken, smitten by God, and afflicted."

- *"He was oppressed and He was afflicted, yet He opened not His mouth."*
- *"He was led as a lamb to the slaughter."*
- *"He was taken from prison and from judgment."*
- *"He was cut off from the land of the living."*
- *"They made His grave with the wicked."*
- *"He was numbered with the transgressors."*

To illustrate this, I'll share a story concerning a family member. When a relationship begins between a young man and young women there are dreams envisioned and a growing love that is very invigorating. As a parent, when you see this begin to happen you are excited about their newfound love. But then there comes a day when that relationship gets strained for various reasons and there comes a breakup. As a parent you can't help but suffer with your loved one because you care about their well-being. If I were to see my loved one going through the things listed above, I would be extremely sorrowful. Fellowship with Jesus' sufferings is not just an emotion felt. In order to suffer with Him, we must drink the same cup as He drank. Jesus said we would not be loved by the world if we loved Him. In following Jesus we will suffer the same experiences listed above that He suffered. We will be despised and rejected by men. We will be esteemed smitten and afflicted. If we are despised and rejected by man, those looking on will see us as afflicted and most likely ignore us. We also will be led as a lamb to the slaughter. In prison for His sake; judged; cut off from the living. We will be numbered with transgressors because evil will be good and good will be considered evil as has happened in this present day. So when you ask to be like Jesus or even to be a ruler with Him, be prepared to drink of the cup that He drank from and to be baptized with His baptism. Jesus summed it up in one sentence: *"If they have called the master of the house Beelzebub, how much more will they call those of his household!"* (Matthew 10:25) If the world hates you just remember it hated Jesus before it hated you. If you love the world, the world will love you because you are like them. If you love Jesus, you are not like the world and those that love the world will hate you. So be aware of your own prayers and requests from God, because He will ask you if you are able to drink of His cup.

"For which of you, intending to build a tower, does not sit down first and count the cost, whether he has enough to finish it -- lest, after he has laid the foundation, and is not able to finish, all who see it begin to mock him." (Luke 14:28-29) If we consider the cup and then drink it, we must be able to finish what the cup has brought into our lives. Before Jesus spoke about building a tower, He makes a statement that is most chilling and can never be taken lightly. He said that whoever does not bear his cross and come after Him cannot be His disciple. A cross is not an affliction, disease, sickness, or failed business deal. A cross kills those who carry it!

REWARDS
January 23, 2016

"What will a man give in exchange for his soul?" Matthew 16:26

      This verse has been very mysterious to me over the years. How can a man give something for his own soul unless he gives his time, strength, and energy pursuing the thing that he desires? I believe the verses before and after the one mentioned above give the key to answering this. Jesus said in verse 24 that anyone desiring to come after Him had to deny himself and take up his cross. In other words he would be denying his own soul and exchanging it for a cross coming along side of Jesus with His. Jesus also said that whoever desired to save his life would lose it. This would mean not exchanging your soul for the cross but keeping it in pursuit of the good things that the world has to offer. The exchange for our soul happens in the moment we decide to pursue the very thing that we have our eye on. This thing could be the whole world, as Jesus mentioned, or it could be losing our life for His sake. Then Jesus ties it all together with these words: *"The Son of Man will come in* *the glory of His Father with His angels, and then He will **reward** each according to his works."* (Matthew 16:27) What will be the works revealed when He comes? Will it be the pursuit of this world's goods or will it be the pursuit of a cross? Jesus doesn't just leave us with the end result mentioned. He is very gracious and kind and gives us a teaser to invoke us to forsake the pursuit of the world and desire greatly to follow Him. We see this on the Mount of Transfiguration. After He has said all of the above He tells those following Him that there are some who will see Him in His glory. Peter, James and John were the ones that observed these very things. On this mountain He presented a glimpse of the reward of those who would decide to exchange their soul and the pursuit of the world with a relentless pursuit of Himself! There are great rewards for those who walk this way.

There is another passage of Scripture that mentions great rewards to those who would pursue them. Psalm 19:11 says, *"Moreover by **them** Your servant is warned, and in keeping **them** there is great reward."* (emphasis mine) Through *them* we are warned yet also encouraged to keep *them*. When it says "*them*" what does it mean? Before we look at what *them* is, we must look at the life of David. David, a man after God's heart, was the author of this Psalm. He knew what pleased God and because of this, God gave Him a forever promise (reward), which has been recorded multiple times in Scripture.

- *"And your (David's) house and your kingdom shall be established **forever** before you. Your (David's) throne shall be established **forever**."* (2 Samuel 7:16)
- *"I will establish one shepherd over them and he shall feed them--My servant David. He shall feed them and be their shepherd."* (Ezekiel 34:23)
- *"David My servant shall be king over them, and they shall all have one shepherd." . . .and My servant David shall be their prince **forever**."* (Ezekiel 37:24-25)
- *"For to us a Child is born, to us a Son is given. . .Of the increase of His government and of peace there shall **be no end**, upon the throne of David."* (Isaiah 9:6-7 AMP)

- *"You will prolong the king's life. He shall abide before God **forever**. I will sing praise to Your name forever, that I may daily perform my vows."* (a Psalm of David 61:6-8)
- (all emphasis above is mine)

What were David's vows? I believe his vows are directly related to *them*! We find *them* in Psalm 19:7-9: The Law, the testimony, the statutes, the commandment, the fear, and the judgments of the Lord. David says in these there is great reward. I know what some of you might be thinking right now; "We are not under the Law! We don't live in fear! We are not under judgment!" David seemed to think that everyone of these was very important in the life of a believer. David was looking for rewards! Notice what it says about each one of these mentioned.

- *"The law of the Lord is perfect, converting the soul."* The law has no flaws or imperfections so it completely and marvelously changes ones life. Reward!
- *"The testimony of the Lord is sure, making wise the simple."* Reward! Enough said!
- *"The statutes of the Lord are right, rejoicing the heart."* Statute means permanent rule. David said it caused his heart to rejoice. Reward!
- *"The commandment of the Lord is pure, enlightening the eyes."* If our eye is evil as Jesus said, then our whole body is full of darkness. If we love Him we will keep His commandments and then our eye will be good and our whole body will be full of light. Keeping His commandments gives entrance to our body being full of light because they enlighten us. Reward!
- *"The fear of the Lord is clean, enduring forever."* It's clean -- no evil! Reward! Enough said!
- *"The judgments of the Lord are true and righteous altogether."* We can look at the judgments of the Lord one of two ways. Either God is an angry person who can't tolerate disobedience or God is so perfect and pure in His Fatherhood that discipline emanates from His very being. Reward!

Every judgment is founded completely and unconditionally in righteousness, holiness, and purity. No evil intent!

Another place in Scripture that addresses rewards is in 1 Corinthians 3:9-17. Here Paul says there is no other foundation that we can establish because that foundation has already been laid; Jesus Christ. He goes on to talk about those who build on that foundation and the materials that they will use. Some will build with fire-tempered materials such as gold, silver, precious stones. Others will build on that foundation with fire consuming materials such as wood, hay, and straw. As we build upon this foundation we are establishing the temple of God. We are building God's house and Paul calls himself a wise master builder. All who name the Name of the Lord will build on this foundation adding to God's house, some being wise and some being foolish. It all depends on the materials that are used. Verse 13 explains that each one's work will become clearly known, because the Day of the Lord will declare it. Fire will test everyone's work that has been built upon that foundation. If our work has large amounts of selfish ambition, worldly pursuits, and impure motives we are building with wood. If our work has unchecked sinful desires or secret sins hidden from man and God, we are building with hay. If we want to perform miracles, cast out demons, and prophecy yet don't want His Lordship in our lives, we are building with straw. Guess what happens to these materials when fire gets on them? Paul says the fire will first test each ones work to see what kind of work it is. Then the fire will burn it, completely consuming it if it hasn't already been fire tested. You can see why it's so important to build with fire-tested materials (an overcoming lover of God and His Word)! Here is the reward part:

> *"If anyone's work which he has built on it endures, he will receive a reward."* (verse 14)

Fire-tested material will always endure! God loves giving out rewards! It's His most desirable pleasure!

Jesus also received rewards: *"Who for the joy that was set before Him endured the cross, despising the shame, and has sat down at the right hand of the throne of God."* (Hebrews 12:2) Yes

Jesus endured the fire of the cross and it was through that enduring that He sat down at the right hand with joy inexpressible.

I would like to end this chapter with a very sobering note. Up to this point we have addressed God's temple; the building that we are helping to build by our works and labors of love of which we will be rewarded. We have also addressed what happens if we build with the wrong materials. I find verses 16 and 17 of 1 Corinthians 3 to be very serious in the light of God's kingdom. God is addressing each one of us individually regarding these verses. *" Do you not know that you are the temple of God and that the Spirit of God dwells in you? If anyone defiles the temple of God, God will destroy him. For the temple of God is holy, which temple you are."* This is the reason why we must build with fire-tested materials. If we are careless in our walk with the Lord and become lawless, yet still naming His name while we sanction things directly against His word, we are defiling His temple. If we carelessly walk through this world and indulge and participate in it and then pretend to build on the foundation with fire-tested materials, knowing they are not, then we are defiling His temple. If we neglect to overcome as Revelation 21:7 encourages us to do, then we enter the list in verse 8 which once again speaks of fire and the result of it's burning. *"But the cowardly, unbelieving, abominable, murderers, sexually immoral, sorcerers, idolaters, and all liars shall have their part in the lake which burns with fire and brimstone, which is the second death."*

Beloved, He has given us everything that pertains to life and godliness and will always lead us in triumph in Christ. How can we not be an overcomer awaiting our reward!

THE WORLD IS SUFFERING AN INVASION
January 29, 2016

      Words, words, words! The world is filled with words! Words cover the face of the earth and words fill every valley and rest on every mountaintop. Words are in the ocean depths and extend to the outer most limits of the universe. Words fill our homes, schools, markets, workplaces, streets, cities, and nations. Words, words, words! There are words of business and an abundance of words in advertisements. There are words between friends, lovers, and even haters. We have words for our pets and special words for when we smash our thumb using a hammer! In all these trillions upon trillions of words spoken, what about the voice -- the still, small voice. The small voice that said in the beginning, *"Let there be light!"* The small voice that still speaks that same thing today. He has not raised the decibel level of His voice. His words are still as powerful today as they were in the beginning. The problem that we face is how to sort out His words from all the rest. In this day of who can have the loudest voice, we find screamers and yellers, complainers and skeptics, those that speak very loving words to their pets, yet curse, swear and excoriate scathingly their very own children. The advertisements we hear tell us what we want, what we need, and how to get it. They also tell us, in detail, about our sickness or disease and what we can purchase to fix it. They say that when we obtain their product we will feel so much better -- it's as if God Himself has touched us! Yes they don't say those words, but they insinuate by their words this very message. Don't get me started on the process of electing a president. One man cannot save our country!

One man can save the world and His voice has been heard from the beginning! He has spoken and we have heard Him, yet His voice is drowned out by screamers and yellers. He has spoken but we have been to busy listening to other voices that we don't hear Him anymore. I cannot emphasis enough that the voice of the Lord has spoken to everyone that lives on this planet. He has spoken to Hitler, _____, _____, _____, (you fill in the blank) and many other men and women that most would label to be evil and wicked people. You might ask how has He spoken to them? Listen to the words of Jesus in John 6:44-45. *"No one can come to Me unless the Father who sent Me draws him . . . It is written in the prophets, **'And they shall all be taught by God.'** Therefore **everyone** who has heard and learned from the Father comes to Me."* (emphasis mine) Didn't Jesus just say that God taught *all*? He also said that everyone who listened and learned from God would eventually come to Him. All of us hear Him speak, but we all do not listen and learn. What was our heart response to His voice throughout our childhood and into our adult years? Even in our darkest most sinful moments He is speaking to us. We will either listen to Him or listen to all the other voices -- strangers, friends, our own, or even the voice of the evil one. Who are you listening to? His voice always leads us to Jesus and repentance. We can't have Jesus without repentance.

How do we know when it's His voice speaking and not our own? We won't unless we have a standard to measure by. A standard that is permanently fixed as an anchor that is solidly placed and will not be moved. This anchor is the Bible! I see many that rejoice in the fact that they have the Holy Spirit in their lives and they trust Him to give them words of encouragement, words of prophetic utterance, or even words to direct their very own lives. The Holy Spirit does lead us into all truth and is our teacher, but we still must have an anchor holding us to the foundation. What is the foundation? Have you read through the book of Jeremiah lately? Ninety-five percent of the book of Jeremiah is God's voice speaking. He is speaking very clearly to all who would hear Him. I point this out because Jesus also knew this as He walked this earth. As a boy He learned to hear the voice of God through listening to the writings of men like Jeremiah, Isaiah, and Moses. These books were read in the synagogues and Joseph and Mary took Him there regularly. While in the synagogue, Jesus would hear words like the following taken from Isaiah 42:14-17: *"I have held My peace a long time, I have been still and restrained Myself. Now I will cry like a woman in labor, I will pant and gasp at once. I will lay waste the mountains and hills, and dry up all their vegetation; I will make the rivers coastlands, and I will dry up the pools. I will bring the blind by a way they did not know; I will lead them in paths they have not known. I will make darkness light before them, and crooked places straight. These things I will do for them, and not forsake them. They shall be turned back, they shall be greatly ashamed, who trust in carved images, who say to the molded images, 'You are our gods.'"* These words express the very heart of God towards His people. Jesus heard these words also and received them deep into His very being because He knew He was to be the fulfillment of them. On that silent night in Bethlehem it wasn't just Mary crying out in labor; God, the Father, was doing the same!

    God has heart responses in the same way that we have heart responses, of which we call emotions. His responses come from a heart that has no evil intent or selfish desires. His desire is for us and for our good, and Jesus Himself has expressed this desire: *"Do not worry about your life, what you will eat or what you will drink; nor about your body, what you will put on. Is not life more than food and the body more than clothing? Look at the birds of the air, for they neither sow nor reap nor gather into barns; yet your heavenly Father feeds them.* ***Are you not of more value than they?"*** *(emphasis mine)* As God was expressing Himself through Isaiah in the above paragraph, He was proclaiming to His people the same message as He did through Jesus. My paraphrasing goes like this:

"You are more valuable to Me than birds and I will come upon you so very strongly that all the mountains and hills in your life will be wasted to nothing! You who are blind I will lead you through darkness and crooked places. I will open your eyes with blinding light so that you will be ashamed of what you have given yourself to. This thing I will do for you!"

Hosea 11:8-10 also speaks expressly concerning the Father's heart for His children. *"My heart churns within Me; My sympathy is stirred. I will not execute the fierceness of My anger. . . For I am God, and not man, the Holy One in your midst; and I will not come with terror. They shall walk after the Lord. He will roar like a lion. When He roars, then His sons shall come trembling."* They will come trembling not in terror but with great respect. They tremble because they hear His voice! When someone truly hears His voice they can't help but tremble. If we don't tremble then we haven't heard. I know some of you will take up issue with that statement saying that He is our Daddy and not just our Lord. I must ask you, didn't you tremble in your earthly dads presence when you knew he wasn't happy with your actions or responses? Even our earthly dads knew what was best for us. Remember, our dads were not like our heavenly Father; they had wicked, sinful, evil hearts; yet even in their weakness, they knew we could do better. When we tremble at God's word it shows that we have a healthy fear of the Lord. Did you know that Scripture says the opposite of the fear of the Lord is to be a fool? Proverbs 1:7, *"The fear of the Lord is the beginning of knowledge, but fools despise wisdom and instruction."* This is the very key to hearing His words/voice. His voice brings wisdom for living, and His words bring instruction to be able to walk out His wisdom in the fear of the Lord. We will notice, in the Bible, that there is a pattern of response from those who hear the voice of the Lord. All these listed below fell on their faces after having an encounter with God. If we have never fallen on our face or even shed one tear after we read the Bible, we must ask ourselves if we even have a relationship with Him.

Abraham (Genesis 17:3)
Moses (Exodus 3:6, Numbers 16:4, 20:6)
Joshua (5:14)

David (2 Samuel 12:16)
Ezekiel (1:28, 3:23)
Daniel (10:8-11)
Peter (Luke 5:8)
Mary (John 11:32)
Paul (Acts 9:4)
John (Revelation 1:17)
Ananias (Acts 5:5) He didn't fall down as dead, he was dead!
The 24 elders (Revelation 4:10, 5:8,14)
The angels and the four living creatures (Revelation 7:11)

It isn't just the faithful that hear His voice and fall down. The willfully unfaithful and the wicked will hear and also bow as Philippians 2:10 says: *"At the name of Jesus every knee should bow, of those in heaven, and of those on earth, and of those under the earth."* If we love Jesus we will obey Him. Obedience is the determining factor between those who are faithful and those who are unfaithful.

STUMBLING BLOCK
February 3, 2016

Subtitled: The Hypocrites Hot Button!

Imagine if Jesus was walking the earth today and He invited you into His home for dinner. Upon your arrival He invites you in, you sit down, and He asks you what you would like to drink. He gives you several options -- beer, margarita, bloody Mary or just wine? Making this observation you would have to infer that Jesus had a wet bar in His house. To some this would not be a surprise, because they also have a wet bar in their house. Yes, they invite other believers over for fellowship and maybe even a Bible study and don't even think twice about trying to justify their bar. It is acceptable to them and to God -- He doesn't care. Even Jesus drank wine would be the quick response of those who imbibed in intoxicating drink. I must ask, when Jesus made wine at the wedding in Cana and those who tasted it said they had kept the best wine till last, was this wine fermented? Did Jesus take care to add the fermentation process to the water He had just turned into wine?

You can argue this, but knowing Jesus' desire to have a holy people we must conclude that it was sweet wine -- not fermented.

This topic is a very hot button for believers in this day. They would rather fight than switch, to use an old commercial quip. They are completely convinced that drinking is an acceptable social decision, no matter where they are or who they are around. They would also be adamant to tell you that it is not really addressed in the Bible except in Ephesians 5:18 where it says, *"Do not be drunk with wine, in which is dissipation."* Most interpret this to say that someone should not over indulge; know your limits. The word dissipation does mean an act of self-indulgence, but if you look at the word dissipate it means to use up wastefully; gradually vanish. So if you drink and do get drunk, you dissipate. Does this mean you use up the wine wastefully so that it gradually vanishes, or does it mean you waste and use up gradually the desire for God, holiness, and purity for which He has poured out His Spirit upon you. In the Amplified Bible the word debauchery is used instead of dissipation. The word debauchery means extreme indulgence, orgies, seduction from virtue. The very term "seduction from virtue" should make us run from any kind of intoxicating drink. I know that I have not convinced some of you on this subject so I must share some Scriptures and let you decide if they are relevant for you or not.

In 1 Peter 2:5 it says *"You also, as living stones, are being built up a spiritual house, **a holy priesthood**, to offer up spiritual sacrifices acceptable to God through Jesus Christ."* (emphasis mine) Plainly stated, we are a holy priesthood! A priest stands before God and offers up sacrifices to God on behalf of himself and others. Another Scripture that mentions us as priests is in Revelation 1:5-6 which states *"To Him who loved us and washed us from our sins in His own blood, and **has made us** kings and **priests** to His God and Father."* (emphasis mine) Plainly stated again, we have been made priests of God. We are no different than the priests of the Old Testament except for our sacrifices. We go into the Holy of Holies just like the OT high priest, but what we offer to God is our spiritual sacrifices through praise, prayer, and worship on behalf of ourselves and others. We will be doing this forever. In light of these Scriptures mentioned, we must take seriously what God has called us to be. That being said, we must look at priests in the OT and capture God's heart as He speaks to them about holiness.

    The first encounter between priest and God is in Leviticus 10:1-11. We see Aaron's two sons, Nadab and Abihu which were priests along side their father. To set the stage for this story we must look at Leviticus 9:22-24. Moses and Aaron had just offered the sin offering, the burnt offering, and the peace offering. They went into the tabernacle and came out to bless the people. When they had come out God's glory fell and the people saw it and fire preceded from the Lord consuming the sacrifice. All the people who saw it fell on their faces. Then it says that Nadab and Abihu took their censers with fire in them and put incense on them and offered this fire to God. God had not commanded them to do this thing so the fire that came out from the Lord devoured them. Was this simply an act of disobedience or was there another factor involved? Moses told Aaron what the Lord had spoken to him saying: *"By those who come near Me I must be regarded as holy; and before all the people I must be glorified."* (Leviticus 10:3) It was at this point that the Lord spoke to Aaron saying, **"Do not drink wine or intoxicating drink**, *you, nor your sons with you, when you go into the tabernacle of meeting, lest you die. It shall be a statute forever throughout your generations,* **that you may distinguish between holy and unholy**, *and between unclean and clean."* (10:8-10 - emphasis mine) This seems to be very clear that this command was given directly after the incident with Nadab and Abihu. It could be concluded that they had been drinking and were not able to properly discern the mind of the Lord, thus they were killed. This must be taken seriously if we are to distinguish between the holy and the unholy. Drinking alters our perspective. God also speaks this same thing through Ezekiel in chapter 44:21, *" No priest shall drink wine when he enters the inner court."* To the wise saint this should be enough to make us reconsider our drinking habits. But I must also reveal what God said through Isaiah in chapter 28:7, *"They also have* **erred through wine**, *and through intoxicating drink are out of the way;* **the priest and the prophet have erred** *through intoxicating drink,* **they are swallowed up by wine**, *they are out of the way through intoxicating drink;* **they err in vision**, *they stumble in judgment."* (emphasis mine) This is a picture of some believers that I know personally. They are swallowed up by wine! There is no discernment in their lives. They have no idea the day and the hour that we live in! Their judgment is twisted and they cannot distinguish between what is holy and what is profane. This is a very sad state to be in. I pray their eyes will be opened before it's to late.

You who desire to follow the Lord with your whole heart, you must take these next Scriptures seriously. God wants us to be completely separated for His purposes and for His glory. God spoke to Moses about any man or woman who desired to consecrate themself. It was in regard to taking a Nazirite vow in order to separate himself to the Lord. He would abstain from drinking wine and similar drink. He goes on to describe abstinence not just from fermented wine or drink, but also from grape juice (sweet wine). God loves the Nazarite! This love is also portrayed in the book of Daniel. I can't prove that Daniel was a Nazarite, but he did abstain from wine. *"Daniel purposed in his heart that he would not defile himself with the portion of the king's delicacies, nor with the wine which he drank."* (Daniel 1:8) We know that Daniel had the ability to interpret dreams and was praised for his insights. He was taken captive to Babylon and had his manhood removed from him, but he still determined not to defile himself. God's response to Daniel is recorded in 10:11and 19, *"O Daniel, man greatly beloved."* God expressed His love for Daniel and placed him in a position of authority in order for Him to speak to kings. God looks for someone who's heart is completely sold out to His purposes. Anyone who loves the world is an enemy of God. This world is filled with wineries and brewery's that continue to spew out their venom to all who desire drink. To all who desire the buzz. We look at the wineries as if they have some kind of magical allurement to a better life. House after house filled with wine racks ready to serve. In God's reality, the vineyard is for fellowship that He might partake of its sweet fruit. Jesus talked much about the vineyard in the context of His desire to partake of the sweet wine of fellowship. We know that Jesus only did what pleased the Father. If God changed His attitude towards wine and strong drink when Jesus came then He is very wishy-washy and His word can't be trusted no matter what He says.

THE TIME IS 3AM
February 9, 2016

I was awake and thinking about the things that I have been reading in the book of Daniel over the past few days. It's at this time that God dropped a word into my heart that troubled me, but yet gave me assurance that He really does care about His people. So in the next paragraphs I will endeavor to write down the things that He spoke to me.

Daniel was a young Jewish man that had dreams just as we all do in growing up. He lived in Israel around 2600 years ago. Just around the time of the fulfillment of Jeremiah's prophecy concerning Israel coming under judgment and going into captivity in Babylon. God had raised up Babylon for this very purpose just like He had told Moses who recorded Deuteronomy 28 concerning the blessings and the curses that would come upon Israel depending on their obedience or disobedience to His word. Israel as a nation chose to disobey His word and so the curse of Deuteronomy came in its fulfillment. Daniel, along with many others, was enslaved and carried off to Babylon to live in a foreign land under foreign laws with foreign people as neighbors. On top of all of this, he was also castrated according to Babylonian law and became a slave in Nebuchadnezzar's kingdom. He interpreted Nebuchadnezzar's dream, which referred not only to his own kingdom, but to other kingdoms that would come after his. The dream revealed a stone cut out without hands that came and crushed all of these kingdoms and then filled the whole earth. Daniel interpreted this for the king but was made aware that God had given him understanding so that they wouldn't be killed, as all the others would have been for not knowing the dreams interpretation. (Daniel 2:30) The dream dealt with the destruction of the kingdom of Babylon (Iraq), the destruction of the kingdom of Persia (Iran), the destruction of Greece (Alexander the Great; Europe), and then the Roman empire (Europe). All of these kingdoms that ruled over the entire earth at one time have been destroyed except one. The toes of the feet of the image that Nebuchadnezzar saw in his dream are ten kings that arise in the final days. (Daniel 2:43-44, AMP) Their kingdom has not been destroyed as of yet.

Daniel chapters 7-12 speak of things that will come in the last days. Within these visions of which Daniel spoke, he saw horrendous things that would happen in the world and to his people. Several times Daniel was left with a sense of helplessness and despair. After each occurring vision Daniel expressed himself with grief and trouble. *"I, Daniel, was grieved in my spirit within my body, and the visions of my head troubled me."* (7:15) *"As for me, Daniel, my thoughts greatly troubled me, and my countenance changed; but I kept the matter in my heart."* (7:28) *"And I, Daniel, fainted and was sick for days; afterward I arose and went about the king's business. I was astonished by the vision, but no one understood it."* (8:27).

Beloved, the visions that Daniel received have not been fully fulfilled as to this day. If these visions greatly troubled Daniel, they also should be troubling us because we live in those very days that Daniel envisioned. We will notice what Daniel's response was after seeing all these things: *"I set my face toward the Lord God to make request by prayer and supplications, with fasting, sackcloth, and ashes. And I prayed to the Lord my God, and made confession . . . we have sinned and committed iniquity, we have done wickedly and rebelled."* (9:4-5) We see Daniel's response in regard to these visions and we know that these visions most likely refer to the times we live in, yet they don't seem to trouble us enough to cause us to set our face to seek God and His mercy as Daniel did. We continue just as those who lived in the days of Noah; eating, drinking, etc. We empathize with Daniel in his responses, yet we do a disconnect when it comes to the reality that these things will be effecting us, our children or our children's children. I speak for myself in these things. It's almost as if we live in a non-reality; nothing will effect us because we live in America the greatest country on earth. I would remind you and myself that Babylon fell, Rome fell, and so did many other nations. We, as a nation, are not exempt. I say this with fear and trembling knowing how far we have fallen from God in this country of purple mountain majesty and amber waves of grain. America, America, God shed His grace on thee -- but is it there now? Thank God, Jesus knows us in our weakness as people. He loves us in the midst of all of our wickedness and rebellion and does still desire to shed His grace on us. We must respond just as Daniel did when observing what's coming!

CONSIDER THIS
February 24, 2016

In this day of Spirit-filled believers, we have come to the conclusion from teachings or otherwise, that in order to deal with the devil we must pray loudly in tongues, bind him up, cast him down, and command him to leave us alone and never bother us again. We believe this with all of our hearts because we have seen so many preachers, pastors, and prophets function in this way. I don't see this in Scripture. Yes, God uses every weak thing that we will give Him, but in truth He wants us to grow in grace and knowledge of Jesus Christ. Before you come to the conclusion and say that I'm off base please consider the following:

Luke 4:1 says that after Jesus was baptized He was filled with the Holy Spirit and then went into the wilderness to be tempted by Satan. Notice He was filled with the Spirit! In other words, He experienced the "Day of Pentecost" way before the disciples did. While He was in the wilderness, Satan tempted Him for forty days. Every time He was tempted, He answered with *"It is written."* He had a workable knowledge of the Word of God which He received as He spent time in the synagogue every Sabbath Day from His youth. Luke 4:16 actually says it was His custom to be in the Synagogue on the Sabbath and to stand up and read from the Scriptures. So, if He was in the synagogue from the time He was five years old until He was thirty, He would have been there an accumulation of 1300 days! And depending on how long the service went He would have been hearing the Word of God anywhere from 1300 hours to somewhere around 2600 hours if it was a two hour service. I would conclude from this that an on going workable knowledge of the Word of God is so very important in dealing with temptation and the Devil.

    I said all of this to say this one simple thing: Jesus didn't rebuke, command, pull down, or bind up the Devil; He simply told Satan what God had said! He did command the Devil directly on a couple occasions; once to Peter (Matthew 16:23) and also during His temptation (Luke 4:8). This was His proclamation to him; ***"Get behind Me, Satan!"*** What would this mean in reality today if we were to tell someone to get behind us? Wouldn't it say "Get out of my face and follow me!" Or in Satan's case "Stand in my shadow because I'm pressing into God and all that He has for me!" We cannot say this authoritatively unless we have heard God's voice. Jesus heard God's voice every time He was in the synagogue. I want to walk as Jesus walked, and hear God like Jesus heard God, don't you?

ALSO, CONSIDER THIS
February 24, 2016

How many times have we heard a sermon or read a book based on these Scriptures:

"Then Jesus said to His disciples, 'If anyone desires to come after Me, let him deny himself, and take up his cross, and follow Me. For whoever desires to save his life will lose it, but whoever loses his life for My sake will find it.'" (Matthew 16:24-25)

We all have our own idea of what our cross looks like. I would like to present that Jesus wasn't addressing our personal cross but something far different. You will notice what happened just before Jesus said these things (verses 21-23). Jesus had been telling His disciples that He must go to Jerusalem and suffer by the hands of the religious rulers and then be killed and resurrected. Peter, having concern for Jesus, said that these things should never happen! Jesus, seeing that Peter was siding with Satan, rebuked Satan and also Peter for only being concerned about the things of men and not God. All

Peter had heard when Jesus was addressing them was that He would be killed. Their King would be killed! On the other hand, Satan was hearing that He not only would be killed, but that He would also be resurrected. The resurrection did not register with Peter. Satan immediately responded and Peter sided with him because that was what he had always done up to that point. Satan was trying to derail Jesus thinking he could abort a resurrection! Jesus addressed Satan because he was the problem. He said, *"**Get behind Me Satan!** You are an offense to Me, for you are not mindful of the things of God, but the things of men."* (emphasis mine) We must conclude from this that when Jesus said, *"Whoever desires to save his life will lose it,"* was addressing that our desire to save our life was to agree and side with Satan. Satan's desire is to make us mindful of the things of this life: comfort, pleasure, security, etc.; but in reality he wants to abort our resurrection. Listen to what Amplified says about losing our life:

*"Then Jesus said to His disciples, If anyone desires to be My disciple, let him deny himself **[disregard, lose sight of, and forget himself and his own interests]** and take up his cross and follow Me **[cleave steadfastly to Me, conform wholly to My example in living and, if need be, in dying also]**. For whoever is bent on saving his **[temporal]** life **[his comfort and security here]** shall lose it [eternal life]; and whoever loses his life **[his comfort and security here]** for My sake shall find it [everlasting life]."* (emphasis mine) We side with Satan so much in our everyday life because we are always choosing comfort over the cross (certain death) and security (financial and personal protection) over abandonment to God (a life of faith)! Satan is interested in us having comfort and security because then we don't need God! What is more prevalent in society today than comfort and security, which God seems to be taking away from us little by little. He desires our faith as Jesus expressed in Luke 18:8, **"When the Son of Man comes, will He really find faith on the earth?"** (emphasis mine)

WHAT IF?
February 25, 2016

What if God wrote a letter to America? What would it say?

> "To the angel of the church of America write, These things says the Holy One, the Coming One, the revealer of the secrets of the hearts of all men:
>
> 'I know your deeds, and that you love My presence in your midst, and that you cannot tolerate unfaithful men. I know that you love the less fortunate and have compassion on those who struggle with life controlling problems. I see your desire for My return and for My kingdom to reign on earth.
>
> Nevertheless I have a few things against you, because you have allowed comfort and pleasure to take the place of My presence. You have allowed fullness of food to take the place of fasting. The

desire for a word from "the prophet" has consumed the desire to meditate on and hear My word, which I have preserved for you in a Book. Your endless search for fortune and fame has left you in the desert places dry and empty, because you could not embrace anonymity. You have replaced the marriage bed with abomination, perversion, and pornography. You have become a stumbling block to all the little ones, thus a millstone will be tied around your neck and you will be thrown into the sea.

I am still giving you time to repent, because I'm not willing for anyone to perish.

To him who overcomes . . .
(God has His promises in Revelation 2-3).

He who has an ear, let him hear what the Spirit says to the churches.

QUESTION ASKED
March 6, 2016

    At the beginning of Matthew chapter 24, Jesus' disciples asked Him privately as to when they would see the sign of His coming. Did they know what they were asking when they asked Him this? It seems to me that they didn't have a clue that He was leaving! Jesus begins to expound to them concerning the days that were coming, leading up to the end of the age. He doesn't address their question immediately. Then He says something that would make the hair stand up on those who live by the positive confession; He says, *"All these are the beginning of sorrows."* The beginning of sorrows? That means there are many more sorrows that are coming and He hasn't addressed the sign of His coming yet! What is Jesus thinking? He is suppose to come and deliver us from all sorrow!

    Jesus then begins to speak of tribulation and being hated and betrayed. He speaks of how we must endure to the end to be saved. What is Jesus thinking? Then He speaks of the abomination of desolation and fleeing to the mountains; and great tribulation and woes to the pregnant woman; what is Jesus thinking? Then He says something that made men tremble; *"Unless those days were shortened, no flesh would be saved!"* Jesus still has not addressed their question of the sign of His coming. He then speaks of false christs and prophets who are sent to deceive God's very people into believing a lie. He ends His discourse with the words: *"Immediately after the tribulation"* and then speaks of the sun darkened and the moon not shining and the stars falling and the heavens shaken! What is Jesus thinking? We are suppose to be gone by now! Raptured! Taken! Caught up in the clouds! Forever with the Lord! And yet after saying all of these things that will come to pass in the last days before His return He finally addresses their question. **"Then!"** Finally after all these things have come to pass ***"the Son of Man will appear in heaven!"*** (emphasis mine) It is at this time, after all the sorrows have taken place, that He will come in the clouds with power and great glory sending His angels to gather together all of His elect from one end of heaven to the other. I would have to say at this time that if you think Jesus made a mistake in the order of events, you should re-read Matthew 24 and Luke 21.

REVELATION 9:21
March 19, 2016

Have you ever asked this question regarding Revelation 9:21:

> Why are there only four sins recorded in this last days verse: murders, sorcery, sexual immorality, and thefts?

There are so many more sins (or commandments not to sin) recorded in Scripture that it makes you wonder why only these four sins are brought out. In regard to the happenings of this present day, I will endeavor to explain why only four.

We must remember that this observation takes place directly after one-third of mankind is killed, which happens in the 6th trumpet judgment.

Within the events that precede the recording of four sins, we are going to see tremendous devastation to the earth and to the people of the earth. Imagine for a second what life would be like with one-third of the population of people dead and missing. This would be a major blow to the world's economy, travel, communication system, eco-system, water system, food production and the list goes on and on. People would also be dealing with the stench and air quality because of dead bodies (literally billions), along with dead animals, birds, fish, all wildlife; plus the smoke from burning bushes and trees and many other items that would be very toxic. I'm sure by now you get the picture of life on earth after this event. I could say authoritatively that man will have lost all hope and become very, very desperate. This could be the reason for receiving the mark in order to buy food, which would be very scarce. Then within the confines of this scenario, we have the prediction of Islam's messiah coming to save the planet. It says in the Koran that he will come because of great chaos on the earth. [1]

In observing all this, we notice that it is pointed out in verse 20 and 21 that the rest of mankind who were not killed did not repent. In other words, they just continued doing what they had already been doing. Today, we are seeing four major sins: murders, thefts, sexual assaults, and sorcery as Numbers 24:1 describes. *"Now when Balaam saw that it pleased the Lord to bless Israel, he did not go as at other times, to seek to use sorcery . . . "* He was offering sacrifices to God on altars of Baal in order to curse Israel. Islam is out to curse Christianity and they talk to their god Allah about it. They believe they are talking to the Living God! We are seeing these four sins lived out specifically in the major refugee crisis that has hit the planet.[2]

You will notice in the article from New Year's Eve in Germany that there were numerous thefts along with sexual assaults in Germany. This article didn't address the many beheadings and suicide missions that have killed (murdered) thousands of people

---

[1] http://www.inter-islam.org/faith/mahdi1.htm
http://www.frontpagemag.com/fpm/261559/end-world-muhammad-mahdi-coming-dr-majid-rafizadeh
[2] https://en.wikipedia.org/wiki/New_Year's_Eve_sexual_assaults_in_Germany

throughout the world. There has been a mandate issued by the enemy to spread Shari Law throughout the entire earth. This has been happening for some time now. It will not stop until it is set in place just as Zechariah 5:5-11 speaks of. In verse 10 it talks of a basket with a woman inside called wickedness and the plans of building a house for it in Shinar, which is Iraq. It says in verse 11, when the house is ready, the basket will be set there on its base. It must be noted that the world has not gotten any better. Observe, but take heart --- JESUS IS COMING!!!

THE GOSPEL
October 13, 2016

"And this gospel of the kingdom will be preached in all the world as a witness to all the nations, and then the end will come." Matthew 24:14

I often ask myself what exactly is the gospel? Is it Jesus' life, death, resurrection, and ascension? Is it communicated quickly in one sentence; or is the gospel something that must be shared over a period of time? I think the answer is both! We can look at the thief on the cross to say that it was communicated quickly, but we can look at the children of Israel coming out of Egypt after wondering in the desert for forty years and say the gospel was communicated through a long duration of time. It should be noted that the thief on the cross probably had many encounters with Israel's history and how God had spoken to them. He was probably well aware of the prophecies concerning the coming Messiah, so it seems that he would have had knowledge of these things living in Israel. Point being: Was the gospel quickly communicated to the thief?

I know many an evangelist that desires, even sometimes covets, the results of Peter's preaching as recording in Acts 2:14-41 (3,000 souls were added that day). It wasn't just a quick sermon that Peter gave. It was months and years of preaching and preparing the hearts of people for that day. Most often we fail to see that many of these people were living in Judea and in Jerusalem and Peter tells them that they were the ones who crucified Jesus and had Him put to death. These were the ones who cried out for Barabbas to be released and Jesus to be crucified. These people were not randomly rocking out at a music festival, indulging in the flesh, and then suddenly Peter comes and starts preaching to them. They were seeking a Messiah! They were searching the Scriptures for God's will to be done! They wanted freedom from Rome's control and domination! This man, Jesus, called Himself the Christ. However, Isaiah said the Christ would not be attractive or desirable nor of kingly stature (Isaiah 53:2). But, despite what the Scripture said, they rejected Jesus because He was a plain looking, ordinary man just like themselves. Thus, they were the ones who had Jesus crucified! Can you image if the President came to you incognito and began telling you that he was the President, but you didn't believe him. Instead you mocked him, ridiculed him, and embarrassed him to the point that those with you were so sickened by his foolishness that they beat him thinking he was a phony. Then come to find out a few days later that he really was the President. What would your gut feeling be? This was the same thing that happened on the day of Pentecost. The Holy Spirit was convicting these people of sin, righteousness, and judgment just as Jesus spoke of in John 16:8. Their hearts were stricken because they had rejected the very one that they were looking for. This also happened in the book of Exodus. They also rejected what God had given them.

THE GOSPEL ACCORDING TO EXODUS

In the next few paragraphs I would like to present the gospel according to what Hebrews 4:2 says: *"For indeed **the gospel was preached** to us as well as **to them.**"* (emphasis mine) Who are "**them**"? Backing up a few verses to Hebrews 3:16, we see who "**them**" are. *"For **who**, having heard* (the gospel) *rebelled? Indeed, was it not **all who came out of Egypt**, led by Moses?"* (emphasis mine)

The writer of Hebrews has just declared that the gospel was preached to those who came out of Egypt. This declaration of the gospel in the Old Testament is recorded beginning in Exodus 12.

IT'S MORE THAN JUST THE BLOOD

Moses had just presented to Pharaoh the tenth plague that would come upon Egypt. It was a plague that would kill all of the first born in Egypt; from the courts of Pharaoh to the stalls of livestock in Egypt. Israel was told that they should slaughter a lamb putting the blood on their doorposts and lintels (the weight bearing beam above the door). You will notice in Exodus 12:13, that the blood would be a sign for those in the house and not a sign for God so that He would pass over. *"Now the blood shall be **a sign for you** on the houses where you are. And when I see the blood, I will pass over you."* (emphasis mine) This was an act of faith indicating that they believed God and were obedient to what He said. Disobedience would have been disastrous! Most of us stop right here and say, "It's the blood!!!" Yes it is! It's always been the blood of the Lamb! But it is more than just the blood! The lamb that was taken was to be without blemish and a male of the first year; spotless and set apart completely! They were to keep it for four days before it was to be slaughtered. Notice in Exodus 12:7, that it says the blood of the lamb was to be put on the doorposts of their houses **where they are to eat the lamb**. They were to roast the lamb in fire and **eat all of it**. None of the lamb was to remain till morning. If any was left over, it was to be burned with fire. Plus they were to eat it with their belts on, sandals on their feet, and their staff in their hand. The meal was to be eaten in haste!

"You shall let nothing of the meat remain until the morning; and the bones and unedible bits which remain of it until morning you shall burn with fire. And you shall eat it thus: [as fully prepared for a journey]." Exodus 12:10-11 AMP

This is the very thing Jesus told His disciples to do also. *"Unless you eat the flesh of the Son of Man and drink His blood, you have no life in you. Whoever eats My flesh and drinks My blood has eternal life, and I will raise him up at the last day. For My flesh is food indeed, and My blood is drink indeed. He who eats My flesh and drinks My blood abides in Me, and I in him."* John 6:54-56

These things say to us today that we are to eat all of the Son of Man and be clothed and ready for a journey at any moment. We are not only to eat of His blessings, but we are to also eat of His sufferings. We are to follow Him completely! We are to hear and obey Him completely! We are always, as a bride for her husband, to be ready to be with Him! I must say with sorrow that many believers today (some I know personally) have only tasted Jesus and that is where they stay. Jesus is their ticket to heaven while they pursue other interests. This is living a compartmentalized life. Life is lived as though Jesus has His own compartment. Jesus is worshipped and obeyed in church, and then His compartment is deserted and another compartment is entered. An example could be the compartment of secular music. Most music today is void of God! It only points to people, places, and feelings and not God. God can use the secular and I thank Him that He did in my own life. He used a musical rock opera in 1971, written by unbelievers, to draw me to Jesus! He used it, but wanted me to pursue the Person that this production was talking about. If we are not eating the entire Lamb of God, we could be facing something very disastrous! In Deuteronomy 27 and 28, Israel was exhorted to obey the voice of the Lord and observe His commands. To not do so brought a curse. They didn't obey and Babylon came and destroyed Jerusalem and the Temple, carrying off many captives as slaves. Being saved is hearing and obeying, not just tasting. This would be compared to a newborn that has just tasted his mother's milk. If the newborn is healthy, he will be ravenous for more. Have you lost your appetite for more of Jesus? What do you think would have happened to an Israelite family that decided they wouldn't eat the whole lamb even though God had told them to do so? Would applying the blood only on the doorposts have been enough obedience to cause God to pass over? Is confessing Jesus and asking Him to come into your heart enough? It was enough for the thief who was crucified with Jesus, but what if the thief was taken down from the cross and allowed to live out his life? Would his confession be enough to save him if he continued to be a thief?

THE BREAD (Manna from heaven)

The second way that the gospel was preached to the Israelites is in Exodus 16. [In looking into these things you might find many more, but for the sake of time, I will only point out a few.]

"The Lord said to Moses, 'Behold, I will rain bread from heaven for you. And the people shall go out and gather a certain quota every day that I may test them, whether they will walk in My law or not." (Exodus 16:4)

Listen to what Jesus says on this subject. *"I am the bread of life. Your fathers ate the manna in the wilderness, and are dead. This is the bread which comes down from heaven, that one may eat of it and not die. I am the living bread which came down from heaven. If anyone eats of this bread he will live forever; and the bread that I shall give is My flesh, which I shall give for the life of the world."* (John 6:48-51)

Those that ate the manna were denied entrance to the promised land. Notice they **did eat** of the manna, the bread from heaven. But, listen to what Hebrews 4:2-3 says,

"The word which they heard did not profit them, not being mixed with faith. So I swore in My wrath, 'They shall not enter My rest.'"

Jesus says of himself in John's gospel that He is the bread of life. John declares that Jesus was the Word and the Word was God. *"The Word became flesh and dwelt among us."* Man is to live by every Word that proceeds from the mouth of God. This is the way Jesus lived. How can we think we can live by a little manna once a week and enter His rest? Those who came out of Egypt ate the manna, but as Jesus said *"They are dead!"* They ate it, but didn't eat it as coming from God Himself. How can we know the heart of God unless we eat His Word daily! When Jesus said, *"I never knew you"* to a people who prophesied, did miracles, and cast out demons in His name (see Matthew 7:22-23), He was saying they didn't want to know His heart; only His power. Are we fully living the gospel that has been preached to us or have we hardened our hearts and shut our ears to what the Lord is trying to say to us? The way we live our lives and the things that we allow into our lives are the very evidence of what we believe on the inside. The things that we talk about and deem important are the very evidence of what we believe. Will these things withstand the fire on that day or will they be burned up as wood, hay, and stubble? Are we being saved **only as through fire**?

GOD CAME DOWN AND REVEALED HIMSELF

The third way that I will mention the gospel being preached to Israel is in Exodus 19-20 beginning in verse 11,

"And let them be ready for the third day. For on the third day the Lord will come down upon Mount Sinai in the sight of all the people."

What did that look like? First of all they were to prepare themselves for this event. How were they to prepare?
1. They were not to come near the Mountain to touch it.
2. They were to wash their clothes.
3. They were not to come near their wives.
4. They were to be set apart for two days

Remember what John the Baptist was preaching as he was baptizing and calling Israel to repentance: *"Prepare the way of the Lord!"* The preparation was important in order to be ready for what they were about to experience. God was about to reveal Himself to His people!

On the morning of the third day after their preparation, there were thunderings and lightnings, and a thick cloud on the mountain. It was fully engulfed in smoke and fire, and the whole mountain shook. Also, the sound of the trumpet was very loud. The blast of it was long and became louder and louder. Moses then spoke and God answered him by voice. I would have trembled just as the people trembled when they witnessed that sight! God was emphatic that the people and the priests would not come near Him. I'm not sure why

God would have broken out against them if they were to come near; I can only guess at this point. Nonetheless, it would have been a fearful sight! After this tremendous display of power by the Lord, He speaks to Moses who then speaks to the people His commandments. I can only see this in the light of what Jesus said in Matthew 5:17-18 (AMP):

*"Do not think that I came to destroy the Law or the prophets. I did not come to destroy **but to fulfill**. For truly I tell you, until the sky and earth pass away and perish, not one smallest letter nor one little hook will pass from the Law until all things [it foreshadows] are accomplished."* (emphasis mine)

Jesus didn't just come to fulfill the Law in Himself, He came to fulfill it in us also. No other gods! Don't take His name in vain! (Or as AMP puts it, *"Don't use or repeat the name of the Lord your God in vain [that is, lightly or frivolously, in false affirmations or profanely]."*) In other words don't tell stupid Jesus jokes! Keep the Sabbath holy! Honor your mom and dad! Don't murder (or hate), commit adultery (or uncover your neighbors nakedness on the internet), or steal! Don't lie about your neighbor or strongly desire your neighbors STUFF! As Hebrews 8:10 says,

"This is the covenant that I will make with the house of Israel after those days, says the Lord: I will put My laws in their mind and write them on their hearts; and I will be their God, and they shall be My people."

I'm not advocating that we keep the law in order to be saved. But if we love Jesus with all our heart, soul, mind, and strength; we will naturally (supernaturally) keep the law. If we love Jesus, we will love His law also!

The end of the story for Israel was that they stood far away from God and only wanted Moses to speak to them. Isn't this how it is today in most churches? We don't want God to speak to us; only the pastor (because if we don't listen to him there's no penalty). God revealed Himself and had come to test Israel, that His fear might be in them, so that they wouldn't sin. (Exodus 20:20) The sad thing is they didn't want relationship with God because He made them feel uncomfortable. They wanted to be comfortable in their lifestyle. The definition of the fear of the Lord is to give honor and have a healthy respect towards Him; as in a healthy relationship between a father and a son. A father's grace and mercy causes the son to love and draw close. On the other hand a father's discipline and strength causes a son to respectfully fear and obey his dad. How is it between you and your Father? Has the Father's love and mercy become for you a wink at sin and disobedience? If a father only shows love and mercy when a son disobeys, will that son respectfully fear and obey his father? Please get this: *"THE FEAR OF THE LORD IS THE <u>BEGINNING</u> OF WISDOM, AND THE <u>KNOWLEDGE OF</u> THE HOLY ONE IS UNDERSTANDING."* (Proverbs 9:10) In the days we live in, we definitely need wisdom and understanding because much deception is being released into the earth.

In conclusion, there is so much more to the gospel than what is preached today! If we preach the gospel according to what Israel received, maybe there would be less people confessing Jesus while living in greed and immorality. It's no wonder the Church lacks the power of God. True conversions always produce holiness and separation from the world. To know holiness and separation, we must know His laws and commandments. If we have repented from alcohol, drugs, and cussing; but always seek comfort, pleasure, and a relaxing vacation; have we really come into holiness and separation to God? Faith in Jesus (who fulfilled the law) brings true repentance according to what the law speaks. Jesus can only fulfill the law in us because He has fulfilled it! He is the Word made flesh to dwell among us. The Word, meaning God's Voice throughout history, speaking how to live according to His kingdom and His kingdom rules.

A challenge to the evangelist: Try preaching the gospel according to Exodus 12-20 without any references to the New Testament. Paul only had the Old Testament to reference from as did all of the Apostles. How can we have Paul's effective preaching if we don't have Paul's foundation in Scripture?

www.ingramcontent.com/pod-product-compliance
Lightning Source LLC
Chambersburg PA
CBHW061336040426
42444CB00011B/2948